THE SACCO AND VANZETTI CONTROVERSIAL MURDER TRIAL

A Headline Court Case

Headline Court Cases

The Andersonville Prison Civil War Crimes Trial
A Headline Court Case
0-7660-1386-3

The John Brown Slavery Revolt Trial
A Headline Court Case
0-7660-1385-5

The Lindbergh Baby Kidnapping Trial
A Headline Court Case
0-7660-1389-8

The Lizzie Borden "Axe Murder" Trial
A Headline Court Case
0-7660-1422-3

The Nuremberg Nazi War Crimes Trials
A Headline Court Case
0-7660-1384-7

The Sacco and Vanzetti Controversial Murder Trial
A Headline Court Case
0-7660-1387-1

The Salem Witchcraft Trials
A Headline Court Case
0-7660-1383-9

The Scopes Monkey Trial
A Headline Court Case
0-7660-1388-X

THE SACCO AND VANZETTI CONTROVERSIAL MURDER TRIAL

A Headline Court Case

Judy Monroe

Enslow Publishers, Inc.

40 Industrial Road	PO Box 38
Box 398	Aldershot
Berkeley Heights, NJ 07922	Hants GU12 6BP
USA	UK

http://www.enslow.com

Copyright © 2000 by Judy Monroe

Library of Congress Cataloging-in-Publication Data

Monroe, Judy.
  The Sacco and Vanzetti controversial murder trial: a headline court
case / Judy Monroe.
      p. cm. – (Headline court cases)
  Includes bibliographical references and index.
  Summary: discusses the trial of Nicola Sacco and Bartolomeo Vanzetti,
two Italian immigrants who were tried and convicted for a murder that
they did not appear to have committed.
  ISBN 0-7660-1387-1
  1. Sacco, Nicola, 1891–1927—Trials, litigation, etc.—Juvenile literature.
2. Vanzetti, Bartolomeo, 1888–1927—Trials, litigation, etc.—Juvenile literature.
3. Trials (Murder)—Massachusetts—Juvenile literature. [1. Sacco, Nicola,
1891–1927—Trials, litigation, etc. 2. Vanzetti, Bartolomeo, 1888–1927—Trials,
litigation, etc. 3. Trials (Murder)] I. Title. II. Series.
  KF224.S2 M58   2000
  345.73'02523—dc21
                                                            99-050540

Printed in the United States of America

10 9 8 7 6 5 4 3 2 1

To Our Readers: All Internet addresses in this book were active and appropriate
when we went to press. Any comments or suggestions can be sent by e-mail to
Comments@enslow.com or to the address on the back cover.

Photo Credits: Boston Public Library, Print Department, pp. 3, 10, 14, 37, 45,
51, 81, 94; Library of Congress, Prints and Photographs Division, pp. 18, 28,
55, 63, 69, 75, 83, 88, 91.

Cover Photo: Boston Public Library, Print Department

Contents

1 The Arrest of Sacco and Vanzetti 7

2 America in the Early 1900s 11

3 The Road to Court 24

4 The Case for Massachusetts 41

5 The Case for Sacco and Vanzetti 59

6 The Decision 79

7 Where Do We Stand Today? 85

Questions for Discussion 96

Chapter Notes 98

Glossary 104

Further Reading 108

Internet Addresses 109

Index 110

chapter one

THE ARREST OF SACCO AND VANZETTI

SOUTH BRAINTREE— Murder occurred not once but twice, in broad daylight, on the afternoon of April 15, 1920. At about 3:00 that afternoon, Frederick A. Parmenter and Alessandro Berardelli, were walking down Pearl Street in South Braintree, a small town in Massachusetts. Both men worked for the Slater and Morrill Shoe Factory. As the paymaster, Parmenter handed out the wages in cash to the factory workers each week. Berardelli was Parmenter's guard.

April 15 was payday and Parmenter and Berardelli were headed for the shoe factory. They carried two metal boxes that contained almost sixteen thousand dollars in cash—wages for the workers.

Meanwhile, two men wearing dark clothes and capes watched as Parmenter and Berardelli passed by. Then, one of the caped men grabbed at Berardelli. The second man fired his pistol, putting three bullets into Berardelli and one into Parmenter. Parmenter stumbled and was shot again. Berardelli was hit with two more bullets.

As the men lay dying in the gutter, a third bandit jumped out from behind a pile of bricks. The three men grabbed the payroll boxes and scooted into a nearby getaway car. Two other men were already in the seven-seat Buick.

The car sped off, only to stop as crossing gates were being lowered at a railroad crossing. Waving a pistol, one bandit ordered a railroad employee to raise the gates. The gates were raised and the car barreled out of town. Police cars soon gave chase. One of the bandits smashed the car's rear window and poked a shotgun through, while another threw out strips of rubber with nails embedded in them. The nails punctured the tires of the some of the police cars.

Suddenly, the getaway car spun around and headed back into town. Then it disappeared down a country road in a thickly wooded area. At that point, the police officers lost the getaway car.

Investigating the Crime

The actual crime had taken less than one minute. Chief Michael Stewart and his men immediately began to investigate. They questioned people near the scene of the crime. Some witnesses said that the bandits were Italian. A fur-lined cap was found on Pearl Street near the crime scene on the evening of April 16—more than twenty-four hours after the shooting. It was rumored that this cap belonged to Nicola Sacco. The police also asked local garage owners to be on the lookout for a large Buick or any Italians who tried to get a car. Two days later, the getaway car was found in the nearby woods.

On May 5, 1920, the police got a telephone call from Mrs. Simon Johnson. Her husband owned a garage in nearby Bridgewater. She explained that four Italian men were at her husband's garage. They wanted to pick up an old stored car. Mr. Johnson had refused, pointing out that the car needed current license plates. Two of the men left on a motorcycle. The other two walked several blocks to catch a streetcar. They were Nicola Sacco and Bartolomeo Vanzetti.

The Arrest

Based on Mrs. Johnson's tip, two policemen got on the streetcar and soon found Sacco and Vanzetti. The police arrested them and both were searched. Vanzetti was carrying a loaded .38 Harrington and Richardson revolver and some loose ammunition. Sacco had a loaded .32 Colt automatic and extra ammunition. Tucked into one of Sacco's pockets was a notice announcing a meeting to be held on May 9. Sacco had planned to take the notice to the printer. Written in pencil, in Vanzetti's handwriting, it said:

> Fellow Workers, you have fought all the wars. You have worked for all the capitalists. You have wandered over all countries. Have you harvested the fruits of your labors, the price of your victories? Does the past comfort you? Does the present smile on you? Does the future promise you anything? Have you found a piece of land where you live like a human being and die like a human being? On these questions, on this argument, and on this theme the struggle for existence, Bartolomeo Vanzetti will speak. Hour—day—hall. Admission free. Freedom of discussion to all.[1]

When Sacco and Vanzetti asked the police why they had been arrested, they were not told the real reason. Instead, they were told that they were "suspicious characters."[2] When they were taken to the police station, they were not told why. And when the two were imprisoned that evening, they still were not told why. Neither man had a criminal record or had been arrested before.

Sacco's and Vanzetti's basic constitutional rights had been violated; they had not been told why they had been arrested. Their case would become the most politically charged murder case in the history of American law. Sacco and Vanzetti were believed to be victims of bigotry, or prejudice, based on their Italian heritage and their political beliefs. The notice in Sacco's pocket identified the two men as anarchists. Anarchists are opposed to any type of government. Their arrest coincided

with a time of great political repression in American history. This was called the Red Scare of 1919–1920, when the federal government arrested thousands of foreign-born people throughout the country whose political beliefs differed from what was accepted by the majority of Americans. The Massachusetts murder case of Sacco and Vanzetti lasted from 1920 to 1927.

Sacco (right) and Vanzetti were arrested on May 5, 1920.

chapter two

AMERICA IN THE EARLY 1900s

AMERICA—When Nicola Sacco and Bartolomeo Vanzetti were arrested in 1920, many of the nations of the world were undergoing major political and economic changes. Governments and citizens were reacting to these changes. Some of the upheavals and issues would affect Sacco's and Vanzetti's case.

End of World War I

World War I (WWI) (1914–1918), was called the Great War. The fighting was mostly in Europe, among most of the world's great powers.

The Allies and Central Powers fought over economic and territory issues. In particular, the German empire tried to establish itself as the greatest power in Europe. By the time the bloody war ended, about 10 million people had been killed. At least double that number had been wounded.

The war brought great change to many nations, including the United States. In addition, some European governments were destroyed. The large Austro-Hungarian Empire had dissolved, and Germany was in the midst of upheaval. Russia had gone through a revolution, too. In March 1917, the Romanov dynasty was overthrown. In November 1917, the Bolsheviks, or Russian communists, seized control of the government. Communists support the common ownership and sharing of labor and products. Such massive changes in Europe and Russia led to waves of immigrants—large numbers of people leaving their native countries to relocate—mainly in the United States.

But in the United States, returning soldiers and new immigrants found a weak economy that led to unemployment. Big business ruled the economy. And President Woodrow Wilson, "displayed little regard for the rights of anyone whose opinions differed from his own."[1] When WWI ended, the Wilson administration's attacks on civil liberties increased, especially against communism.[2] For example, during 1919–1920 police throughout the country raided the homes of suspected Communists and made thousands of arrests. Many of these searches and arrests were

OPPOSING POWERS IN WORLD WAR I	
Allies	France, Britain, Italy, United States, and Russia. The United States entered World War I in 1917.
Central Powers	Germany, Austria-Hungary, and Turkey

made illegally. Sometimes search warrants were delivered after people had been arrested. At other times, prisoners were forced to march through the local streets wearing handcuffs.

Civil unrest, such as race riots, strikes (work stoppages), and violent crime, spread across the United States. The industrial states of New England, especially Rhode Island and Massachusetts, were hard hit by a series of armed robberies between 1919 and 1920. To find out what was happening at home and elsewhere, many people read newspapers. Newspapers were affordable and available to most people. People also turned to the radio for news. (Television had not yet been invented.)

Anarchists in America

After the Bolshevik takeover in Russia, Communist terror—also called Red or radical terror because Communists are sometimes called reds—influenced some Americans. Radicals, it was rumored, planned to overthrow the United States government. Radicals advocate extreme measures to retain, restore, or overthrow an existing government.

Americans tended to lump together various radical groups such as Communists and anarchists. Yet these two groups hold different political views and different objectives. For example, anarchists are opposed to any type of government, law, and private property. Their theory is that all forms of government are bad and should be abolished, or removed, so that all people could live in equality. Respect, liberty, and cooperation, not competition, would guide people. In contrast, communism is based on a type of government that enforces the common ownership of the means of production and common sharing of labor and products.

Many anarchists, who were against war in general, opposed WWI.[3] Opposition to America's participation in WWI was considered to be treason—disloyalty to the government.[4] During WWI, President Wilson had set up the Creel Committee on Public Information. This Committee asked Americans to report to the Justice Department in Washington, D.C., anyone "who . . . cries for peace, or belittles our efforts to win the war."[5] Also established were the Espionage Act of 1917, the Trading-With-the-Enemy Act of 1917, the Sedition Act of 1918, and other measures.

Few Americans, including Attorney General Mitchell

Palmer, head of the United States Department of Justice, knew the differences between Communists and anarchists. The Justice Department, part of the executive branch of the federal government, handles cases in federal matters and interprets and enforces federal laws.

During the early 1900s, as a way to protest against the United

Boston's police chief Michael E. Stewart ordered the arrest of Sacco and Vanzetti.

States government, anarchists were responsible for a series of bombings in New York City, Boston, Milwaukee, Philadelphia, San Francisco, and other large cities. Anti-radicals, or people against radicals, began to target anarchists just after America joined the War in 1917. Throughout the country, anti-radicals beat up anarchists and destroyed their homes, libraries, and clubhouses.

In 1919 a new wave of bombings targeted eight cities across the United States. Some of these bombs went off simultaneously in different cities. This time, the bombs were hand-delivered to the intended victims. Many of these bombs were linked to Italian anarchists. Why did they resort to bombings? According to one source, these men were "at war with the forces of government and capital[ism]; and if they resorted to bombs . . . it was for the purposes of war."[6] The targets of these bombs were important political figures such as judges, politicians, and high government officials who had been involved in violating the civil rights of anarchists.

One hand-carried bomb was targeted for Attorney General Palmer. On the evening of June 2, 1919, someone delivered a bomb to his home in Washington, D.C., but it went off too early. Palmer's house shook, all the windows shattered, and the front of his house blew up. Palmer, his wife, and neighbors were not hurt. However, the person carrying the bomb was blown to bits. Sergeant Burlingame, in charge of the bomb investigation, said, "We could not take a step without seeing or feeling the grinding of a piece of flesh."[7] Based on what was left of the bomber's body, the police concluded the person had been a tall Italian man with curly black hair.

The investigators also said the bomber was probably a radical, possibly an anarchist.[8] They came up with this theory because scattered over the bomb scene were printed flyers called "Plain Words." It was signed "The Anarchist Fighters."

The bombs, whether mailed or hand-delivered, heightened the fear of both the authorities and the general public. Widespread fear and paranoia against immigrants, radicals, communists, and anarchists in America resulted.

Red Scare in America

Attorney General Palmer ordered raids to find all radicals—Reds and anarchists—in America. These raids were called the Palmer Raids. Many of the searches and arrests were conducted illegally. Some foreign-born people were deported, or returned to their native country. Others were jailed or put into makeshift camps and held for long periods. Many of these so-called radicals were not granted constitutional rights. They were arrested without search warrants and were not appointed lawyers. This period of panic over radicals in the United States was called the Red Scare. By the time the Red Scare ended in 1920, Palmer's people had made thousands of arrests in dozens of cities. Palmer explained why he had ordered this large-scale sweep for radicals: "Each and every adherent [believer] of this [Red] movement is a potential murderer or a potential thief. . . . "[9] According to Palmer and others, anarchists and Reds were working to spark a social revolution in the United States, similar to what happened in Russia in 1917.

Anti-Immigrant Mentality in America

From 1880 to 1915, millions of European immigrants came to America. Many became manual laborers, including quarry, shoe, cigar, and garment workers. Others became miners, barbers, tailors, bricklayers, and machinists. Some helped form or became members of America's first unions (groups that helped to improve conditions for workers). Some of these European immigrants brought anarchist beliefs to the United States. America stopped the flow of immigrants when Congress passed the 1918 Immigration Act. This law stopped the entry and allowed for the deportation—or return to their native country—of aliens, including anarchists, who supported the use of force to overthrow the United States government. This law and other laws passed at this time helped to limit immigration, especially from eastern and southern Europe.

After the war ended, Boston and nearby towns such as South Braintree had become heavily populated by recent groups of European immigrants. In some areas, more than half of the population was foreign-born. Some Americans saw these people as a threat.[10]

Some immigrants living in Massachusetts were thought not to believe in capitalism or democracy. They were assumed to follow anarchism, communism, or socialism. Socialism is a movement calling for public ownership of factories and other means of production. Since Sacco and

As head of the United States Department of Justice, Mitchell Palmer ordered raids as a way of finding radicals—Reds and anarchists—in the United States. His order triggered the period known as the Red Scare.

Vanzetti were Italian immigrants and anarchists, during their trial, some Americans would see them as a double threat.[11]

Nicola Sacco

Both Sacco and Vanzetti were immigrants. Born in 1891, Nicola Sacco grew up in Torremaggiore, a quiet town in southern Italy. He dropped out of school after the third grade and went to work for his father in the family's olive orchards and vineyards. In 1908, seventeen-year-old Sacco followed a brother to America. He settled in Massachusetts. He first worked as a laborer but soon was hired as a shoemaker at the 3K Shoe Factory in Stoughton. A hard worker, Sacco earned a decent salary in his trade. He regularly sent money to his family back in Italy and set up a savings account for them.

Michael Kelly owned the 3K Shoe Factory. Kelly trusted Sacco and sometimes hired him as a night watchman for the shoe factory.[12] Kelly later said of Sacco, "A man who is in his garden at 4 o'clock in the morning, and at the factory at 7 o'clock, and in his garden again after supper and until nine and ten at night, carrying water and raising vegetables beyond his own needs which he would bring to me to give the poor, that man is not a 'holdup man.'"[13]

In 1912 Sacco married Rosina, an Italian immigrant. A year later the couple had a son, Dante. During free time, the Sacco family went on picnics to the nearby countryside or to the seashore of the Atlantic Ocean. Soon after Sacco was arrested, his daughter, Ines, was born. One of Sacco's letters, written in his limited English, described his love for his family: ". . . some time Rosina she youst halp me to carry him in that same time she youst get Dante in her arm both of us youst give him a warm kisses in is rosy face. Those day . . . they was a some happy day. . . ."[14]

While in America, Sacco had grown increasingly upset with the "injustice and cruel persecution in this free society today, and specially for the poor people."[15] By 1913 he had become involved with an anarchist group. For Sacco, anarchism was a "noble faith," and he was determined to fight and even die for his beliefs.[16] Sacco had not come to America as an anarchist. But the many poor people he saw and talked with regularly influenced his decision to accept anarchist beliefs. To help fellow workers, Sacco participated in union strikes. He and his wife acted in plays to raise money for the anarchist movement. He also subscribed to and wrote articles for anarchist publications.

As an anarchist, Sacco opposed World War I. In 1917 he fled to Mexico because he did not support the war effort. He returned to Massachusetts a year later and resumed his old job at the 3K Shoe Factory.

Bartolomeo Vanzetti

Bartolomeo Vanzetti was three years older than Nicola Sacco. Vanzetti grew up in the town of Villafelletto in northern Italy where his father was a prosperous farmer. Vanzetti attended school until the age of thirteen. Then his father put him to work in a bakery. Like Sacco, he came to the United States in 1908. For the next nine years, he worked as a laborer doing many different jobs. He washed dishes in restaurants, then became a bricklayer, a woodcutter, a ditchdigger, a telephone installer, a stone carrier, a cook, and finally, a factory worker.

Although Vanzetti never returned to school, he read and studied throughout his life. "Ah," he said, "how many nights I sat over some volume by a flickering gas jet, far into the morning hours."[17] He read about many subjects such as world history, philosophy, literature, science, religion, and politics.

Never married, Vanzetti was a close friend of several families and many young people. He rented a room for four years with the Brini family. The youngest member of that family, Beltrando Brini, became Vanzetti's "spiritual son."[18] Vanzetti would "pay attention to me in the instruction of the Italian language or in my playing the violin or in my school work," Brini recalled.[19]

Vanzetti's interest in anarchism developed from three sources. First, he took to heart what he learned from reading. Second, he drew upon his own experiences as a manual worker—the low pay, hard labor, and crowded rooming houses in which he lived all helped shape his beliefs. Third, from talking with fellow workers and finding out how they dealt with their own poverty and difficult situations, he came to support anarchism.

By 1912 Vanzetti had become involved with an anarchist group. He went to anarchist meetings, made speeches, and collected money for the anarchist cause. Like Sacco, he subscribed to and wrote for anarchist publications. Also like Sacco, he went to Mexico in 1917 because he did not support the war effort during WWI. He, too, returned to

Massachusetts after the war ended. To earn money, he sold fish, clams, and eels from a handcart. He also began the process of becoming an American citizen.

Sacco and Vanzetti—Anarchists

Sacco and Vanzetti met and became friends while planning to go to Mexico. After returning to Massachusetts, they joined the same group, the East Boston Anarchists. This group met every Sunday afternoon. Sacco and Vanzetti continued their commitment to anarchism. Sacco told his daughter, Ines, "The nightmare of the lower classes [workers] saddened very badly your father's soul."[20] Vanzetti explained, "Both Nick [Nicola Sacco] and I are anarchists—the radical of the radical."[21]

Sacco and Vanzetti belonged to a militant (violent) branch of anarchy. These anarchists preached revolt against government by violence, including the use of bombings and assassinations. Before equality and justice could exist in America, they said, the government needed to be overthrown—by violent means if necessary.[22]

Sacco and Vanzetti were very active for their cause. They distributed anarchist pamphlets and flyers and participated in demonstrations. Both men wrote for and subscribed to *Cronaca Sovversiva*, an anarchist newspaper. As a result of their anarchist activities, Sacco and Vanzetti, along with the other members of their anarchist group, were being investigated by the United States government.

During 1919 through 1920, the Red Scare was in full force. Newspapers carried stories about anarchists who had been jailed or sent back to their native countries. Some anarchists fled the United States. The police had arrested and jailed some of Sacco's and Vanzetti's anarchist friends, and reports had circulated that some anarchists had died while in jail. One of their friends, Andrea Salsedo, had supposedly revealed the names of other anarchists before apparently jumping out of the window in his jail cell in New York City. He died as a result of injuries from the fall. Due to increasing pressure by the government against anarchists living in the United States, Sacco and Vanzetti began planning to return to Italy.

On March 23 or 24, 1920, Sacco received a letter from a brother in Italy. His brother had sent bad news—Sacco's mother had died. Come home, said his father. Kelly, his employer, gave Sacco time off from work to visit the Italian Consulate in Boston on May 4. Sacco returned the same day with a passport to Italy.

Meanwhile, Vanzetti had moved into Sacco's home to help pack the family's belongings. On May 5, Sacco and Vanzetti, along with two other anarchists, went to pick up a car at Johnson's garage in Bridgewater. While returning by streetcar, police arrested them.

chapter three

THE ROAD TO COURT

COURT HOUSE—When they were handcuffed on May 5, 1920, Nicola Sacco and Bartolomeo Vanzetti thought they were being arrested for their anarchist activities.[1] There were three reasons for this belief: First, the police never told them that they had been picked up for questioning about robbery or murder. After all, they had never hidden their anarchist views and many activities related to their cause. In Sacco's pocket at the time of their arrest was a notice about an anarchist meeting. Second, the police focused their questions on Sacco and Vanzetti's political beliefs and activities. Third, neither Sacco nor Vanzetti had any previous criminal record.

So when questioned after their arrest, Sacco and Vanzetti lied about their political beliefs and activities to protect themselves and their anarchist friends from possible consequences of the Red Scare. The two men were not informed of their rights, including the fact that they did not have to answer any questions asked by the police. In 1920, they did not legally have to be informed of their rights.

The First Night

Shortly after their arrest on May 5, at 11:00 P.M., police chief Michael Stewart questioned the two men. According to official records, when Stewart asked Sacco and Vanzetti about their political beliefs, they did not tell the truth. They both denied that they were anarchists.

Both also lied about why they had gone to South Braintree earlier that day. They said they intended to visit a friend. Then they told more lies. They denied knowing the other two men who had also tried to get the car that was stored at Johnson's garage. They were dishonest about their guns and told lies about how long they had owned them and from whom they had bought them.

Chief Stewart never told the two men why they had been arrested. Neither Sacco nor Vanzetti was told that they were being held on suspicion of murder and robbery. Chief Stewart never mentioned the April 15 crime in South Braintree. Instead, the police focused their questions only on the radical anarchist activities of Sacco and Vanzetti.

The two men were locked in cells for the night. Sacco decided that their arrest was connected with their anarchist activities or for draft dodging. Sacco came to this conclusion "because [he] was working for the movement for the working class, the labouring class," he later said.[2]

Since there were only bare wooden boards to sleep on, Vanzetti asked for blankets. The officer refused and said, "tomorrow morning we put you in a line in the hall between the chairs and we shoot you."[3] At this point, a police officer loaded his gun, then pointed it at Vanzetti who did not flinch.

Questioned by the State District Attorney

The next day, Massachusetts District Attorney Frederick Katzmann came to question Sacco and Vanzetti. No account was written to document Katzmann's questions and Sacco's and Vanzetti's responses. For this reason, no record exists of what actually happened. Some of the alleged exchanges between the three men came out later at the trial.

Based on the trial records, Sacco and Vanzetti gave false or unclear answers to some of Katzmann's questions. By law, the district attorney is responsible for telling suspects—people who are thought to have been involved in a crime—why they were arrested. Yet at no time did Katzmann tell the two men that they were being held on suspicion of the South Braintree murders, as testimony by Vanzetti later revealed. For example, when he was asked if Chief Stewart or District Attorney Katzmann told him that he was suspected of a robbery and two murders, Vanzetti said no. Why had the police arrested him? Vanzetti said, "I understand they arrested me for a political matter."[4]

Katzmann questioned the two men about their activities on April 15, 1920. Vanzetti said, "Common to every other day to me, I peddled fish."[5] Sacco replied that he had been at work.

The two men were photographed, taken to Brockton

Police Station, and charged with carrying concealed weapons without a permit. Both men pleaded guilty to this charge.

Charged with the Crimes

Later that day, between twenty and thirty witnesses were brought to the jail. They were asked if they could positively identify Sacco or Vanzetti as being involved in the murders. If they could, they would later testify at Sacco's and Vanzetti's trial.

The witnesses, all from South Braintree and Bridgewater, were asked whether the suspects had been at the murders or in the getaway car. The police made Sacco and Vanzetti face the witnesses in a variety of poses. They had to kneel, raise an arm as if using a gun, take off hats, and crouch. These poses were similar to those that the killers had used during the crime. Witnesses could walk around the suspects and see them from all angles. Neither man was put into a formal lineup—a line of people, including the suspect, arranged by the police for identification by witnesses.

Based on what the witnesses said to the police, on May 6, 1920, the *Boston Globe* newspaper reported that Sacco and Vanzetti had been caught carrying guns illegally. This was the first newspaper article about the case of Sacco and Vanzetti.

After Chief Stewart and District Attorney Katzmann pooled their information about the suspects, they filed a case against both men for the robbery and the murders of Parmenter and Berardelli. In a criminal case involving robbery or murder, the state accuses and prosecutes, or brings to trial, suspected criminals. So the state of Massachusetts charged Nicola Sacco and Bartolomeo Vanzetti with armed robbery at South Braintree and with the murders of Alessandro Berardelli and Frederick Parmenter.

Bartolomeo Vanzetti was also charged with attempted robbery and murder for an earlier botched robbery in Bridgewater. When he was arrested, Vanzetti had some shotgun shells in his pockets. These shells may have matched

When Sacco (second from left) and Vanzetti (walking to Sacco's right) were arrested, they denied that they were anarchists.

shotgun shells found at the scene. The Bridgewater robbery involved four men who tried to rob the payroll truck of the White Shoe Company on December 24, 1919. The truck was carrying Christmas wages, in cash, for the factory workers. Although the bandits and security guards exchanged quite a few bullets, no one was hurt. After two minutes, the bandits stopped shooting and sped out of town in a large dark car.

Vanzetti's Bridgewater Case

District Attorney Katzmann asked Judge Webster Thayer to try Vanzetti for the Bridgewater case first. After that trial, Sacco and Vanzetti would stand trial for the South Braintree murders and robbery. Judge Thayer agreed to these trial plans. The Bridgewater trial began on June 22, 1920, in Plymouth, Massachusetts.

Sixteen witnesses, all Italians, testified that Vanzetti had sold them eels throughout Christmas Eve, December 24. (Some Italians traditionally eat eel on Christmas Eve at the evening meal.) According to the witnesses, Vanzetti was busy selling all that day, including during the time of the attempted burglary, which occurred at about 7:30 A.M. on December 24. Each witness needed an interpreter to understand and respond to questions.

On July 1, 1920, the jury found Vanzetti guilty of both charges. "*Coraggio* [courage]," said Vanzetti, as he turned toward his friends.[6] Judge Thayer sentenced Vanzetti to twelve to fifteen years in Charlestown State Penitentiary. He was assigned to make license plates while in jail.

Steps of a Criminal Case

Vanzetti's Bridgewater criminal case followed specific legal procedures. These same procedures were also followed for Sacco's and Vanzetti's South Braintree case.

Although the sequence of steps can vary from state to state, nowadays this is the usual procedure for a suspected criminal case:

Arrest—After police investigate a crime, they file a report describing the crime and naming a suspect. Then the police must find and arrest the suspect. Upon arrest, suspects are informed of their rights.

Booking—At the police station, the suspect is searched, photographed, fingerprinted, and allowed to contact a lawyer. The suspect is sometimes jailed.

Initial Court Appearance—At the initial court appearance, the judge informs the suspect of the charge and his or her rights. The judge also decides if the suspect should be released on bail or kept in jail. Bail is the release of an arrested person in exchange for a promise to appear in court later. The suspect's next court date is set.

Preliminary Hearing—A preliminary hearing is called for a suspect accused of a felony. A felony is a serious crime generally punished by imprisonment. If the judge decides there is enough evidence, the case is forwarded to a grand jury.

Grand Jury Indictment—The grand jury decides if enough evidence exists for the accused to stand trial.

If it votes yes, a court order called an indictment is issued, requiring the suspect to stand trial.

Arraignment—The judge reads the charges to the accused, who is again advised of his or her rights. The accused then pleads guilty or not guilty. If pleading not guilty, a date is set for the trial; guilty, a trial is not held. Instead a date is set for sentencing.

Pretrial Hearing—The judge meets with the attorneys from both sides and reviews the issues of the case.

Trial—The accused, now called the defendant, stands trial before a jury, a group of people who have sworn to decide the facts in a court case and to reach a fair decision. A trial is a formal presentation of both sides of a case before a jury. In a criminal case, the state has the burden of proof. This means the state must persuade the jury that enough facts exist to prove that the defendant is guilty of the crime.

Verdict—After hearing the evidence and testimony in the case, the jury reaches a verdict, or final decision. If not guilty, the defendant is free; guilty, the defendant receives a sentence, or punishment.

Sentence—At the end of a criminal trial, the jury or judge decides the punishment.

Rights of Criminals

If arrested and tried on a criminal charge, several amendments to the United States Constitution protect the rights of the accused. These amendments include many safeguards to ensure that the criminal procedures are fair. In the Constitution, these safeguards are part of the amendments that make up the Bill of Rights. The Bill of Rights consists of the first ten amendments to the United States Constitution. It protects the rights of individuals.

Fourth Amendment
Protects against

- Unwarranted search and seizure of property or person. The person must give permission, or the state must have a search warrant.

- Being arrested without probable cause. Probable cause is when the state can demonstrate that the police knew enough at the time of the arrest to believe that an offense had been committed and that the defendant likely committed it. The defendant is the person accused of committing the crime.

Fifth Amendment
Gives the accused the right to remain silent during questioning, protecting against self-incrimination. This means the accused can refuse to answer questions subjecting him or her to accusation of a crime.

Sixth Amendment
Gives the accused the right to

- A lawyer to represent him or her in court;
- A speedy public trial with a fair or impartial (not biased) jury;
- Be informed of all charges;

- Present witnesses in his or her favor; and

- Cross-examine the government's witnesses. Cross-examination is the questioning of the opposition's witnesses.

Eighth Amendment

Protects against cruel and unusual punishment if convicted and sentenced for a crime.

Pretrial Steps

On May 26, 1920, a preliminary hearing for Sacco was held. No record exists to show that Vanzetti had a preliminary hearing. Also, no record of Sacco's hearing has been published. Based on the trial records, we know that police and witnesses testified at Sacco's preliminary hearing. After hearing the testimony, the judge said that there were reasonable grounds, or probable cause, that Sacco had committed the murders and robbery. Probable cause is strong reason to suspect that Sacco and Vanzetti committed the crimes. Sacco's and Vanzetti's case was sent to a grand jury.

Twenty-three men were selected for the grand jury. (Women gained the right to vote in 1920, but in many states they were still barred from serving on juries.) The men on the grand jury were chosen from voter registration cards. The grand jury hearing was held on September 11, 1920—the earliest possible date following the sentencing of Vanzetti in the *Bridgewater* case. Neither Sacco nor Vanzetti, nor their lawyers, were allowed to attend the grand jury proceedings. The twenty-three men heard only the witnesses who spoke against the two accused men. Then the prosecutor gave a summary of the case. The prosecutor is a government official authorized to accuse and prosecute (bring to trial) someone who is believed to have committed a crime.

That same day, the grand jury indicted both Sacco and Vanzetti for the first-degree murder—murder that was planned before it was committed—of Berardelli and Parmenter. An indictment is a formal, written accusation that outlines what crimes are believed to have been committed. It also names those who probably committed the crime. In Massachusetts in 1920, the penalty for first-degree murder was death.

Sacco and Vanzetti returned to jail. On September 28, Sacco and Vanzetti were arraigned. During an arraignment, the judge reads the charges to the accused. The accused then pleads guilty or not guilty. If not guilty, a trial date is set. Both men pleaded not guilty, and their case was scheduled for March 1921. However, Sacco's and Vanzetti's lawyers requested more time to prepare for the case. The trial was postponed to May 31, 1921. It would be held in the small, quiet town of Dedham, Massachusetts.

The Judge

Before the trial began, Judge Webster Thayer asked to be appointed the judge for Sacco's and Vanzetti's case. He was granted the case despite the fact that he had been the judge at Vanzetti's first trial and may have been biased against the men. During a trial, judges should not take sides. However, Judge Thayer's bias against anarchists was well known in the community.[7] For example, at a ceremony for newly Americanized citizens in 1920, Thayer spoke out against anarchism. In another instance, even before the grand jury had been selected in the Sacco and Vanzetti case, Judge Thayer told reporters that he would "take care of Sacco and Vanzetti" once he instructed the jury on how to decide their verdict.

The duties of a judge include

- Listening to evidence;

- Making certain a defendant's constitutional rights are protected;

- Making certain proper legal procedures are followed; and

- Listening when the lawyers argue over evidence, then deciding, based on rules of evidence, if the evidence should be admitted into the trial.

Jury Selection

Before a trial officially begins, a jury of twelve people must be selected by the judge and lawyers for both sides. This process began on May 31, 1921, for the *Sacco and Vanzetti* trial. All jurors must be impartial, or not biased, against the defendants.

The duties of a jury include

- Evaluating the evidence presented at the trial;

- Deciding if a defendant is guilty beyond a reasonable doubt—the highest level of certainty a juror must have in the court system to find a defendant guilty of a crime;

- Reaching a unanimous decision after hearing all the evidence at the trial; and

- Announcing the verdict, or decision, to the defendant and judge.

Steps would be taken to keep the jurors from having any contact with anyone or anything that might influence them about the trial. To ensure that they stayed impartial during the entire trial, the twelve jurors

- Could not see or talk with anyone about the trial, including immediate family members, and;

- Could not read newspaper articles about the trial.

Between May 31 and June 4, 1921, more than seven hundred men were summoned to the Dedham courthouse as possible jurors. Judge Thayer explained to them their rights and duties about jury service. To eliminate biased jurors, the judge asked each man questions such as if they were related to Sacco, Vanzetti, or the murdered men, or if they were against the death penalty.

The lawyers rejected most of the possible jurors. Many men already knew about the case or had strong feelings against the death penalty. Others found excuses for not serving because they "feared possible revenge of the Reds" or "they didn't want to get mixed up in the affair."[8] In the end, twelve men were chosen as jurors. None of the jurors was Italian, which could have been due to the fact that many of the Italian men were not registered voters at that time, so they could not volunteer to sit on a jury. All jurors were sworn in shortly after 1:35 P.M. on June 4, 1921.

Judge Thayer appointed one of the jurors, Walter Ripley, as the foreperson. The foreperson leads or organizes the discussion of the jury and is responsible for keeping order. Later, it was learned that before the opening of the trial, a friend had told Ripley that perhaps Sacco and Vanzetti were innocent. Ripley replied they "should be hung anyway."[9]

Pretrial Hysteria

From 1919 to 1920, Boston and its many suburbs such as South Braintree were steeped in the "lawlessness and hysteria" of the Red Scare.[10] To many people, Reds included all radicals such as Communists, socialists, and anarchists. Hysteria ran so high that Boston bankers paid for full-page newspaper ads against Reds.

Before he was tried with Nicola Sacco for the murders of Frederick Parmenter and Alessandro Berardelli, Bartolomeo Vanzetti was tried separately for attempted murder and robbery. Standing next to Vanzetti (right) is a prison guard.

In the minds of some people, Sacco and Vanzetti were already guilty because they were radicals—anarchists and draft dodgers. The United States government had been investigating them for some time. As Katherine Anne Porter (1890–1990) explained,

> Anarchy had been a word of fear in many countries for a long time, nowhere more so than in this one [America]; nothing in that time, not even the word "Communism," struck such terror, anger, and hatred into the popular mind. . . .[11]

Porter was an American writer who described her involvement and feelings about the *Sacco and Vanzetti* case in her book *The Never-Ending Wrong*.

After Sacco and Vanzetti were arrested, their anarchist group organized a defense committee. The committee published a pamphlet that described the upcoming trial of Sacco and Vanzetti. It also collected money to help the two men.

Soon other people, not just anarchists, joined the defense committee or helped in other ways. To raise money, they held plays, concerts, shows, and picnics. They also wrote articles and pamphlets. Soon the organized labor movement in America—the unions—heard of the upcoming case and lent their support and contributed money. The American Civil Liberties Union also became interested in the case of Sacco and Vanzetti.

The Media Heightens Interest

National magazines began to publish articles about the case. In December 1920, the *New Republic* magazine published

"Eels and the Electric Chair." This article described Vanzetti's trial in Bridgewater and asked for a review and a reversal of the trial and its sentence.

By spring 1921, interest in Sacco's and Vanzetti's case had spread worldwide, especially among workers' unions and other working-class people. Articles appeared in newspapers in America and around the world. People discussed the upcoming trial in the press, in clubs, in streetcars, and at home. When the trial started in May 1921, hundreds of angry letters about the trial were arriving at the courthouse each week.

Some of the newspapers said that Sacco and Vanzetti were dangerous, gun-carrying Reds. Other newspapers said Sacco's and Vanzetti's case was secretly connected to Andrea Salsedo's arrest and mysterious death. (See page 23 for more information about Andrea Salsedo.) Such speculations brought hordes of news reporters to the trial. Before the trial, steel shutters and steel doors were added to the Dedham courthouse.

Unusually strict security measures were enforced throughout the trial. Five nearby towns lent members of their police forces to protect those in Dedham from Sacco and Vanzetti, whom the press called "dangerous Reds."[12] State troopers along with the local police guarded the entrance to the Dedham courthouse, the halls, and the courtroom. Rows of uniformed police sat in the courtroom.

Although they were not handcuffed during the trial, Sacco and Vanzetti had to sit in steel cagelike enclosures in the center of the courtroom. This was a Massachusetts court custom of that time for those accused in criminal cases. These enclosures were used to prevent the escape of defendants. Deputies watched them constantly. The judge issued instructions that anyone coming into the courtroom be searched for hidden weapons. Whenever Sacco and Vanzetti were brought to and from court, they were handcuffed and surrounded by police.

The strict security, along with the fear and excitement of the trial itself, created a lot of interest from the press during the trial. This, then, was the emotionally charged setting when Sacco and Vanzetti's trial officially began on Monday afternoon, June 6, 1921.

chapter four

THE CASE FOR MASSACHUSETTS

DEDHAM, MA—The joint trial of Sacco and Vanzetti took place in Dedham, Massachusetts, between June 6 and July 14, 1921. As a result of the many people who testified for each side, the trial ran for more than six weeks. The case, officially called the *Commonwealth of Massachusetts* v. *Nicola Sacco and Bartolomeo Vanzetti*, was recorded on thousands of pages, which resulted in six volumes, or books.

The Trial Process

To present the facts, both sides in a trial call witnesses. These people come to the witness stand in court and swear to give truthful testimony or information. Sometimes one or both sides hire expert witnesses. These people have special knowledge of a subject, but no relationship to the case at trial, and are allowed to testify in court. Both sides can also present evidence. Evidence is any physical items relevant to the trial. This can include relevant documents, photographs, maps, guns, bullets, or clothing.

During a criminal trial, both sides—the prosecution, in this case the state, followed by the defense—present their witnesses and evidence to the jury. During this process, witnesses are called to the witness stand, sworn in to tell the truth, then asked questions. Each side calls its own witnesses and questions them on direct examination. This means that they may ask only "direct questions" or open-ended questions that do not suggest a specific answer. "Where were you at 3:00 P.M. on April 15, 1920?" is a direct question.

The prosecuting lawyers present their witnesses and evidence first. The prosecutors try to convince the jury that the defendants are guilty of the charges. The defense then questions the prosecution's witnesses to try to show that the

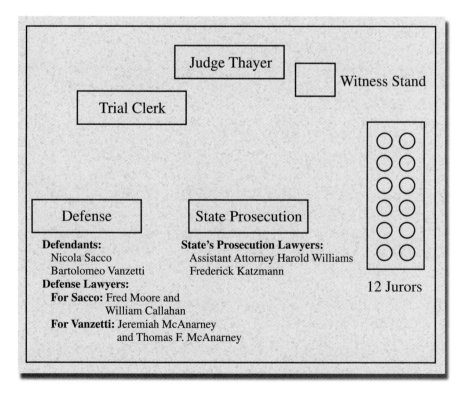

witnesses are not believable, incorrect, or prejudiced against the defendants. This process is called cross-examination.

Defense Lawyers

For Sacco—Fred Moore and William Callahan
For Vanzetti—Jeremiah McAnarney and Thomas F. McAnarney

State's Prosecuting Lawyers

Assistant Attorney Harold Williams
Frederick Katzmann

The Prosecution's Strategy

During the trial, the prosecution attacked Sacco and Vanzetti in three main ways:

- Both defendants could be identified by witnesses.

- Physical evidence, or items of proof, included a so-called cap of Sacco's, his gun and bullets, and Vanzetti's gun. The guns and bullets, said the prosecution, appeared to be the type used in the murders.

- The pattern of Sacco's and Vanzetti's behavior after the murders and robbery showed that they were guilty of the crimes.

The Prosecution's Opening Statement

On Monday, June 6, 1921, the trial of Sacco and Vanzetti officially began with an opening statement by the prosecution. Opening statements summarize the strong points of each side's case and what each side intends to prove during the trial. However, nothing the lawyers say during the opening statement is considered to be evidence.

In his opening statement, prosecutor Harold Williams described the basic facts of the robbery and Parmenter's and Berardelli's murders. He named several witnesses who claimed to have seen the defendants during the crime. He then concluded with the arrest of Sacco and Vanzetti:

> The police arrested the defendants. Sacco had a loaded .32-caliber Colt automatic pistol tucked down inside his pants. He also had twenty-two bullets. Our experts concluded that the bullet that caused Berardelli's [the guard] death was fired from a .32 automatic like Sacco's Colt. Vanzetti had a loaded .38-caliber Harrington & Richardson revolver on him. A cap found near Berardelli's body is similar to Sacco's cap. Both men had known each other for some time before this.
>
> We have direct evidence of Sacco shooting at Berardelli. There is no eyewitness evidence that Vanzetti fired any gun. But evidence put Vanzetti in the car and at the scene of the crime. And Massachusetts law says everyone who took part in this holdup and shooting is guilty of murder as much as if they had actually fired the shots.[1]

Witnesses Testify for the Prosecution

After finishing the opening statement, the prosecution began calling its witnesses to the stand for questioning. Fifty-nine witnesses testified for the state. The state first tried to establish that Sacco did the actual shooting on April 15, 1920. To prove this, the prosecution produced sixteen witnesses who identified Sacco. However, during the trial, only five witnesses definitely identified Sacco as being in the getaway car or on the spot at the time of the murders. They were Mary E. Splaine, Frances Devlin, Louis Pelzer, Lola R. Andrews, and Carlos E. Goodridge.

Mary E. Splaine. Splaine, a bookkeeper, was working on the second floor of the Slater and Morrill factory. Her desk was near a window that overlooked the crime scene. On the day of the murders, she heard a gunshot. Looking out the window, she saw an automobile crossing the railroad tracks. She claimed to have seen Sacco in the escaping car.

Sacco and his wife Rosina are shown leaving the Dedham Courthouse during the trial.

Splaine gave a lot of detail in her testimony. But she only saw the getaway car for a few seconds, from a distance of about sixty to eighty feet. The car was traveling at the rate of fifteen to eighteen miles per hour.

Splaine described the color of the man's shirt, his face, hair color and length, eyebrows, hand size, weight, and complexion. In all, she remembered and described sixteen different details. Despite her many details, on cross-examination by the defense, Splaine admitted that during the preliminary hearing she could not identify Sacco. However, by the end of her questioning in the Dedham courtroom, Splaine did testify that Sacco was the man she saw leaving the crime scene.

She made her identification of Sacco almost entirely on his hands, which she repeatedly said were large. In reality, Sacco's hands were smaller than average for a man of his height and weight.[2]

Frances J. Devlin. Devlin and Splaine were working together when they heard a gunshot. Like Splaine, Devlin jumped up, looked out the window, and saw a car crossing the tracks. At the preliminary hearing, Devlin would not say for sure if she saw Sacco.

Yet over a year later at the trial, she testified that Sacco was the man she saw on April 15. Why had she changed her testimony? Devlin said, "On account of the immensity of the crime and everything, I hated to say right out and out."[3]

Louis Pelzer. Pelzer was a shoe-cutter at the Rice & Hutchins factory, directly across from the location where the murders occurred. He was on the first floor when he heard gunshots. He testified that when he heard shooting, he pulled up his window three or four inches, glanced at the crime scene, and saw the man who killed Berardelli.

But during the cross-examination by the defense, an important fact came out. When he was brought to the jail the night Sacco and Vanzetti were arrested in May 1920, Pelzer could not identify Sacco. Before and during the trial, Pelzer changed his testimony many times. Because of his conflicting statements, he lost credibility as a witness for the prosecution. In fact, District Attorney Katzmann disregarded Pelzer as a witness in his final summary statement to the jury.[4]

Lola R. Andrews. Before the trial, the prosecution said that Andrews was a star, or important, witness. That is because Andrews claimed that she had actually talked with Sacco on the morning of the murders. She testified that about four hours before the murders, she saw two men beside a car parked outside the Slater and Morrill factory. One man had a light complexion. This could not be Sacco or Vanzetti, since both had dark complexions, hair, and eyes. The other man, who was looking inside the car's hood, had the opposite complexion of his companion.

Andrews did not talk to either of the two men. She went into the factory to ask about a job. When she came back out, she again saw the darker man and he was still under the hood of the car. She asked him for directions to another factory, which he gave her, and she left.

At this point, a disbelieving Sacco stood up in the

defendant's cage and said to Andrews, "I am the man? Do you mean me? Take a good look!"[5]

During the trial, Andrews never said anything about the man's strong accent. This is important, because it would have helped identify Sacco. English was Sacco's second language and he spoke and understood it poorly. He also spoke English with a heavy accent.

Andrews identified Sacco when she was brought to the jail the night of his arrest. Again she identified him at the trial. But how did she connect the man with the dark complexion to the murders that occurred four hours later? She said, "When I heard of the shooting I somehow associated the man I saw at the car."[6]

Carlos E. Goodridge. Just after the shootings, Goodridge was coming out of Magazu's Pool Room. In court testimony, he said that he saw the escaping car going past at ten or twenty miles per hour. When a man in the car held up a gun, Goodridge ran back into the poolroom. About seven months after the murders, he claimed that Sacco was one of the bandits in the car. He identified Sacco at the trial.

Goodridge, though, was a crook with a long criminal history of small thefts and skipping bail. In fact, when Sacco was about to begin his preliminary hearing, Goodridge was about to be charged once again with stealing. After the trial, it was discovered that Goodridge was a fugitive from justice in another state and had given evidence under a false name. Because of his unsavory background, Goodridge was not a credible witness.

Prosecution's Physical Evidence Against Sacco

The prosecution spent a lot of time on its physical evidence. This included a cap and Sacco's gun and bullets. Physical evidence, if determined to be genuine during the trial, could be positive proof of guilt. In trials, physical evidence is of a higher order, or more convincing, evidence than witness identification. That is because witnesses can tell lies or become confused and forgetful.

The Cap. The first mention of a cap found near the murder scene occurred on April 17, 1920, in the *Boston Herald*, a local newspaper. This was two days after the murders. The newspaper reported that an employee had found the cap late on the afternoon of April 16, the day after the murders. After the cap was given to the police, the chief of police made a hole in the cap's lining to search for any identification. Before then, the cap had been whole. The size of the cap was never revealed to the jury.

The prosecution first asked George Kelley, Sacco's employer, if the cap belonged to Sacco. Court testimony revealed that Kelley did not identify the cap as Sacco's. No one else identified the cap. Then the prosecution said that the tear in the cap was made from Sacco regularly hanging it on a nail. Neither the prosecution nor defense asked the police about the tear. Later, Katzmann had Sacco put on the cap. It was too small and did not fit properly. The *Boston Herald* noted that "it stuck on the top of his head and he [Sacco] turned with a satisfied air to let the jury see."[7]

The Pistol and Bullets. Sacco owned a Colt .32 caliber automatic pistol. Since the four bullets removed from

Berardelli's body were fired by a .32 automatic, Sacco's gun was suspected as the murder weapon. The prosecution asked Captain William H. Proctor, a ballistics (gun) expert, to examine Sacco's gun and the bullets removed from Berardelli.

Expert testimony, such as that by Proctor, is one of the most important features of a criminal case. The testimony of an expert witness is of higher weight, or more credible, evidence than that of other witnesses.

Proctor, who lived in Massachusetts, was a police captain in charge of a division of state police. He had been a captain for sixteen years and on the force for twenty-three years and was the state's leading ballistics authority. After the murders, Proctor went to South Braintree and tested Sacco's gun by shooting bullets from it. He then compared these fired bullets with the four bullets removed from Berardelli's body. Three of the four bullets, said Proctor, were fired from a Savage automatic pistol—not Sacco's gun.

However, he said, the third bullet could have been fired from the same type of gun as Sacco's, a Colt automatic pistol of .32 caliber. "Why was this?" asked the prosecution. Proctor said,

> This bullet [the third one] has got a left-hand twist instead of right. In the second place, the grooves made by the pistol while through this bullet are .060 of an inch and I don't know of any other pistol than a Colt automatic that gives a groove like that. No other pistol, other than a Colt automatic, gives a left-hand twist or slant to the groove on the bullet.[8]

Yet during a question-and-answer-exchange, when

Proctor was asked if the third bullet came from Sacco's Colt, he first said yes, but later said no.

To make Proctor's testimony sound more credible, the prosecution brought in Captain Charles Van Amburgh, an assistant in the ballistics department of the Remington Union Metallic Cartridge Company in Connecticut. He tested Sacco's gun, then was asked to examine the third bullet. When asked by the prosecution if that bullet was fired from Sacco's gun, he answered, "I am inclined to believe that it was fired . . . bullet No. 3 was fired from this Colt automatic pistol," but he admitted, "I have a slight hesitation [as to whether it was actually fired from Sacco's gun.]"[9]

So after many hours of testimony, the state's two expert

Sacco and Vanzetti (back row center two men) are taken from jail to court. The prosecution presented five witnesses who said Sacco was either in the getaway car or at the scene of the murder.

witnesses could not say for sure if the third bullet taken out of Berardelli's body had come from Sacco's gun.

The Prosecution's Witnesses Against Vanzetti

The state claimed that Vanzetti sat in the getaway car on April 15, 1920. This act made him one of the collaborators in a conspiracy, or plan, to murder. A collaborator is someone who works with others on a plan. To prove this theory, the prosecution produced various witnesses. Only four people identified Vanzetti. Of these, two witnesses claimed that Vanzetti was in the getaway car. The other two testified to seeing Vanzetti the day of the murders.

Between 10 A.M. and noon on April 15, 1920, Harry E. Dolbeare testified that he saw a large car go past him with five people in it. One of the occupants, he said, was Vanzetti. However, under cross-examination by the defense, Dolbeare could not provide details of Vanzetti or anyone else in the car. He could only say that the men "were a tough-looking bunch."[10]

Only one witness, Michael LeVangie, claimed to have seen Vanzetti immediately after the murders. LeVangie was the gatekeeper at the railroad crossing at the time the escaping car passed through. He identified Vanzetti as the driver of the getaway car. But Vanzetti had never learned to drive and did not have a license to drive. Because LeVangie gave many conflicting statements about what he saw after the shooting, he was not a believable witness for the state.

Austin T. Reed was the gatekeeper at a nearby railroad crossing when the getaway car passed through. This was more than an hour after the murders had occurred. Reed claimed to have recognized Vanzetti sitting in the front seat of the getaway car. Reed's testimony did not support the prosecution's claim that Vanzetti was sitting in the backseat. Also, Reed testified that Vanzetti's English was "unmistakable and clear."[11] But in April 1920, Vanzetti could speak very little English.

John W. Faulkner testified that he had seen and talked with Vanzetti on a train at 9:54 A.M. on April 15, 1920. Vanzetti supposedly was headed for South Braintree. When he was cross-examined by the defense, Faulkner admitted that he could not identify Vanzetti from his police photos. He could not identify anyone else on the train that morning, even though he regularly rode that train. Also, for three months after the shootings, Faulkner never mentioned to anyone that he had supposedly seen Vanzetti the morning of April 15.[12]

Prosecution's Physical Evidence Against Vanzetti

When he was arrested, Vanzetti was carrying a loaded .38-caliber Harrington & Richardson revolver. One of the slain men, Berardelli, also owned a .38-caliber Harrington & Richardson revolver. The state tried to prove that during the murders, Vanzetti grabbed and kept Berardelli's gun.

About three weeks before his death, Berardelli had taken his gun for repairs to Iver Johnson's, a sporting goods shop. A spring in the gun had broken. He left the gun with Mr. Wadesworth at Iver Johnson's, after showing him the broken spring. Wadesworth gave a claim check to Berardelli for his

38 Harrington & Richardson revolver. Since it was Parmenter who actually owned the gun, Berardelli later gave him the claim check.

During the trial, three important facts about this gun came out:

- Iver Johnson's employees could not find any record to show that the repaired gun had been paid for and picked up or delivered.

- Iver Johnson's sales manager, Mr. Jones, testified that he could not find a record of the sale of the Berardelli/Parmenter revolver. Unpaid guns left in the shop were sold by Iver Johnson's after a certain period of time.

- Mrs. Berardelli, wife of the slain man, did not know if the repaired revolver ever came back from the shop.

The prosecution, then, could not prove that Berardelli had gotten his repaired revolver from the shop or that he had it on the day of his death. No witnesses could testify if Berardelli had a revolver with him at the time of the murders. Also, no one had seen any of the murderers take a gun from Berardelli.

The prosecution continued to try to show that Vanzetti had pocketed Berardelli's gun. When Vanzetti was arrested, he had lied about his revolver. He was not truthful about how long he had it and where he had got it. The lies, claimed the prosecution, showed that Vanzetti had indeed taken Berardelli's gun.

None of the previous owners of Vanzetti's gun had recorded its serial numbers. Serial numbers are unique for each gun and can positively identify a particular gun. During the trial, all the previous owners were not even sure if this was their former gun. Vanzetti's gun was a common, cheap type and looked like many others readily available. Iver Johnson employees could not positively identify the gun since they had failed to record the serial number.

The prosecution again tried to show that Vanzetti's gun was really Berardelli's revolver by asking George F. Fitzemeyer to testify. Fitzemeyer had been a gunsmith at the

Sacco and Vanzetti are shown as they appeared in court. Even though the state never claimed he fired any shots, Vanzetti was tried because they said he was in the getaway car, making him a collaborator.

Iver Johnson Company for more than thirty years. When asked if any recent repairs had been made to Vanzetti's revolver, he said it had a new hammer. That, however, is not the same as a new or repaired spring.

Guilty Behavior

The state presented another argument that Sacco and Vanzetti were involved in the murders. Before and after their arrest, said the state, both men "behaved exactly as one might expect of two captured murderers."[13] According to Paul Avrich, a history professor and expert on anarchism, Sacco's and Vanzetti's behavior at the time of their arrest weighed heavily against them.[14] The lies that Sacco and Vanzetti had told made them seem guilty of covering up suspicious behavior of their supposed involvement in the robbery and murders.

The state gave five reasons why Sacco's and Vanzetti's behavior proved they were guilty of murder:

- On May 5, Sacco and Vanzetti, along with two other Italian anarchists, went to pick up an automobile at Johnson's garage in Bridgewater. They gave up when told that the car was not licensed for 1920. Why did they leave? The real reason, claimed the prosecution, was that the men saw the garage owner's wife go to a neighbor's house to telephone the police about them.

- When arrested, both Sacco and Vanzetti were heavily armed.

- Sacco's and Vanzetti's guns and bullets appeared to

fit with at least some of the shootings.

- The police claimed that both men tried to resist arrest and that Sacco and Vanzetti were prepared to shoot the police if necessary.

- At the time of their arrest, both men lied about many things, including whom they were visiting and where they had gotten their guns. Anything said at the time of arrest can be used as evidence against the accused.

One of the arresting police officers, on the night of May 5, testified that Sacco and Vanzetti tried to resist arrest and told lies when questioned. For example, when questioned the night of his arrest, Vanzetti claimed to have gone to visit a friend and gave a phony name for his friend. Sacco told the police he was not carrying a gun, but he was lying.

Their guilt kept piling up, said the prosecution. When searched by the police on May 5, both men had loaded guns and ammunition. When they were questioned later that night by Chief Stewart, both men told more lies about why they had gone to South Braintree earlier that day. They claimed that they did not know the other two men who had gone with them to Johnson's garage, how long they had owned their guns, and from whom they had bought the guns. None of these things were true.

Prosecution Ends Its Case

On Tuesday, June 21, 1921, the prosecution ended its case by focusing on two major points: Both Sacco and Vanzetti had been armed during their arrest, and both had lied during their initial questioning. However, at this point in the trial, the stolen money was still missing.

It had taken the prosecution from June 6 to June 21 to present all its witnesses and evidence. Now the defense for Sacco and Vanzetti would present its case.

chapter five

THE CASE FOR SACCO AND VANZETTI

COURT HOUSE—On Wednesday, June 22, 1921, the defense began presenting its evidence and witnesses. The defense represents those accused of a crime (the defendants) during a trial. During a trial, the defense calls its witnesses to the stand to ask them questions. This is called direct examination. The prosecution then can cross-examine defense witnesses. The prosecution cross-examines to try to discredit the witnesses' testimony or show they are not believable.

Ninety-nine witnesses for the defense testified during Sacco's and Vanzetti's trial.

The Defense's Strategy
The defense lawyers were

- For Sacco: Fred H. Moore and William J. Callahan;

- For Vanzetti: Jeremiah J. McAnarney and Thomas F. McAnarney.

Moore was the chief counsel, or the head of the lawyers for the defendants. The defense tried to prove that Sacco and Vanzetti were not guilty of the murders. Their proof had three main parts:

- Witnesses for the defense testified that Sacco or Vanzetti were not at the shootings or in the getaway car.

- Both Sacco and Vanzetti had alibis. Witnesses could place Sacco and Vanzetti elsewhere at the time of the murders.

- Sacco's and Vanzetti's behavior after the murders showed that they were *not* guilty of the crimes. The defense offered explanations of their actions before, during, and after the murders.

The Defense's Opening Statement

On Wednesday, June 21, 1921, the defense began its case with the following opening statement by William Callahan:

> We start the defendant's case at the same place the government opened its case; that is, we presume under law that the defendants are innocent. The burden of proof is still upon the government. The defendants do not have to testify, but they will. They will clear up many points brought up by the prosecution, including why they were armed the night they were arrested.
>
> The defense will be made up of two parts: witnesses who were at or near the scene of the shooting will tell you what and whom they saw. The defendants will explain what they were doing on April 15.[1]

Callahan then gave the names of some of the many witnesses for the defense and briefly explained what their testimony would cover. He continued, "You will learn that several government witnesses said different things before the trial from what they said at the trial. This will make you change your mind about the reliability of their testimony at the trial."[2]

Defense Witnesses for Sacco and Vanzetti

When the defense began calling its witnesses to the stand for questioning, the strategy was to show that the prosecution's witnesses who placed Sacco or Vanzetti at the crime scene were mistaken. To prove this, the defense produced dozens of witnesses who testified that Sacco and Vanzetti were not at the murder site or in the getaway car.

Frank Burke testified that he did not see Sacco or Vanzetti in the getaway car. Burke testified that at the time of the shooting, he saw the getaway car coming toward him. When the car was about ten feet from him, a man in the front seat pointed a gun at him and shouted, "Get out of the way!"[3] Burke said that man was neither Sacco nor Vanzetti.

Just before the shootings, Albert Frantello saw two men on the street. He got a good look at one of the men, and described him in detail at the trial. Frantello, an employee of Slater and Morrill, testified that neither Sacco nor Vanzetti was the man he saw that day.

Winfred Pierce looked out his window just as the getaway car was moving across the railroad crossing. Like Frantello, Pierce worked at Slater and Morrill. At the trial, the defense asked Pierce if either Sacco or Vanzetti was in the car but Pierce could not say for sure.

More witnesses were called by the defense. Among the

witnesses called were laborers who were working about fifty feet from the shooting. These men, Emilio Falcone, Pedro Iscorla, and Henry Cerror, testified that they saw the shooting of Berardelli. All said that the killers were neither Sacco nor Vanzetti.

The only witness who previously knew either of the defendants was Nicola Gatti. Gatti, a railroad worker, knew Sacco for many years. While at work on April 15, 1920, he saw the getaway car leaving the crime scene. Gatti ran toward the car and stopped when he was four or five feet from it. He clearly saw three men inside the car. He described them, then testified that none of these men were Sacco or Vanzetti. Since he knew Sacco, Gatti would have recognized him. Also, Gatti was very close to the getaway car just after the murders.

Contradicting the Prosecution's Witnesses

Other witnesses for the defense directly contradicted testimony given by the prosecution's witnesses that placed Sacco at the murders or in the getaway car.

Thomas F. Fraher Contradicts Mary E. Splaine. As the prosecution's witness, Splaine had testified at the trial that she saw Sacco in the getaway car. Her testimony was already doubtful because she claimed that the man she identified as Sacco had large hands, and Sacco had small hands.

Fraher cast further doubt on Splaine's testimony. Fraher, a supervisor at the Slater and Morrill factory, testified that Splaine was not a credible witness. Fraher was Splaine's immediate supervisor, and he claimed that she was "one of the most irresponsible persons he ever came in contact with."[4]

Contradicting Louis Pelzer's Testimony. Earlier in the trial, Pelzer claimed to have seen the crime as it was taking place. But what did Pelzer really see or do during the shootings? Peter McCullum, William Brenner, and Dominic Constantino, three fellow workers, testified about Pelzer's behavior during the shooting. The four men were working in the same room at the time of the shooting. All said that Pelzer never pulled up the window. Instead, he ducked under a bench when he heard the gunshots. So it would have been impossible for him to have seen anything.

During the time of the Sacco and Vanzetti trial, first degree murder in Massachusetts was punishable by death in the electric chair.

Actually, it was McCullum who opened the window to see what was happening outside. The factory's windows were frosted, or opaque—the workers could not see through them to the outside. That is why McCullum pulled the window up to see what was happening outside. After McCullum opened the window a few inches and peeked outside, he told everyone to get out of harm's way, then instantly closed the window. Pelzer scuttled under a bench right away. He got off the floor only when the other three men got up. Pelzer later told the other men that he did not see any of the shooting through the window.

Contradicting Lola R. Andrews's Testimony. Lola Andrews claimed that she had talked with Sacco on the day of the murders. However, the defense produced four reputable and credible witnesses who discredited Andrews's claim. Those witnesses were Julia Campbell, Harry Kurlansky, George W. Fay, and Alfred Labrecque.

Julia Campbell, a friend of Andrews, had gone with Andrews to ask for a job at Slater and Morrill. Although both women said they had seen a car and two men in front of the Slater and Morrill factory, Campbell contradicted the rest of Andrews's testimony. For example, Campbell testified that they asked for directions from the other man standing near the car (not the man who was working on the car). Further, she said that Andrews had never talked to the man who was working on the car.

Another defense witness was Harry Kurlansky, owner of a small tailor's shop. He had known Andrews for seven or eight years. He testified that sometime in February 1921 he had a talk with Andrews. According to Kurlansky, Andrews told him that when she was asked to positively identify Sacco and Vanzetti, she could not because she said, "I have never seen them and I can't recognize them."[5]

In February 1921, Andrews reported to police that she had been attacked in her Quincy apartment. George W. Fay, a Quincy police officer, investigated Andrews's complaint. While getting the information about the crime, Fay asked Andrews if there were physical similarities between her attackers and Sacco and Vanzetti. She told Fay that she could draw no comparisons because she had not seen Sacco or Vanzetti.

Alfred Labrecque was a newspaper reporter and secretary at the Quincy Chamber of Commerce. He, too, testified that Andrews told him that she had not seen Sacco's or Vanzetti's faces.

Contradicting Carlos E. Goodridge's Testimony. Charles Goodridge had testified that Sacco was one of the men in the getaway car. Four witnesses—Andrew Manganaro, Peter Magazu, H. Arrogni, and N. Damato—contradicted Goodridge.

Goodridge reported that he had supposedly seen his employer, Andrew Manganaro, one hour after the shootings. However, Goodridge did not tell Manganaro anything about the identity of the people involved in the shooting. Then Manganaro testified that he and Goodridge discussed a newspaper article that reported the arrest of Sacco and Vanzetti. Manganaro told Goodridge to go to the police and identify Sacco and Vanzetti. Goodridge refused. What was his reason? He said he could not identify the men he saw on the day of the shooting.

Peter Magazu owned a pool hall. He testified that an hour after the shootings, Goodridge came into his pool hall and briefly outlined the crime. When Magazu asked if Goodridge had seen the killers, Goodridge described one of the men who held a gun. His description did not match either Sacco or Vanzetti.

H. Arrogni was a barber in South Braintree. He testified that about a week after the shooting, he talked with Goodridge in his barbershop. Arrogni told the jury that Goodridge admitted to seeing the getaway car, but he could not identify anyone in it. N. Damato, Arrogni's boss, gave the same information at the trial.

Contradicting the Prosecution's Witnesses

Other defense witnesses directly contradicted testimony given by the prosecution's witnesses that said Vanzetti was in the getaway car or in the area on the morning of the murders.

Contradicting Michael LeVangie's Testimony. Michael LeVangie was the gatekeeper at the railroad crossing at the time the escaping car passed through. While he was lowering the gates, the getaway car drove up to him, and stopped. Michael LeVangie claimed that Vanzetti was driving the getaway car. But there were two problems with LeVangie's claim: Vanzetti had never learned to drive and he did not have a license to drive. Four defense witnesses—Timothy J.

Collins, Henry McCarthy, Alexander G. Victorson, and Edward Carter—also discredited LeVangie's testimony.

Collins arrived at the murder site just after the shooting on April 15, 1920. He was a newspaper reporter for the *Boston Globe* and he interviewed LeVangie. During Collins's question-and-answer exchange, it came out that LeVangie, although he did hear someone yell at him from inside the getaway car, could not describe the driver or passengers. Instead, when LeVangie saw the gun pointed at him, he immediately ran away from the car (toward the gate-keeper's booth). A bullet whizzed by and lodged in the booth.

McCarthy, a railroad fireman, was on a train that stopped for water at South Braintree about forty-five minutes after the murders. Noticing the crowds and an ambulance near the murder scene, McCarthy saw LeVangie and asked him what was happening. LeVangie replied that someone was murdered but that he did not know who had committed the murder. LeVangie, testified McCarthy, said he was unable to describe the men because "all he could see was the gun and he ducked."[6]

Victorson said he overhead LeVangie talking to a group of people about fifteen minutes after the shootings. He testified that LeVangie told the group, "It would be hard to identify these men."[7]

The final defense witness to discredit LeVangie was Edward Carter, who worked at Slater and Morrill. He, too, talked with LeVangie soon after the shootings. LeVangie, said Carter, did see the driver of the getaway car. However, he only gave one detail about the driver—that he was fair-skinned. This description fit neither Sacco nor Vanzetti.

John W. Faulkner Discredited. Faulkner testified that he had seen Vanzetti on a train headed for South Braintree at 9:54 A.M. on April 15, 1920, the day of the shootings. Faulkner's testimony was discredited by four defense witnesses: Henry McNaught, Ernest Pratt, Edward Brooks, and Harry Cash. All of the men worked at the East Braintree railroad station.

Ticket agent Edward Brooks said that he saw a tall, thin man get off the train at East Braintree. He then testified that Vanzetti was not tall. Conductor Henry McNaught said that no cash fares were bought from areas near the murder site on April 15. Pratt and Cash, both ticket agents, testified that no cash fares were sold from areas near the murder site on April 15. Based on these four defense witnesses, said the defense, Vanzetti did not take a train into South Braintree the morning of the murders.

Ballistics Contradicts Physical Evidence

The defense asked two ballistics experts, James Burns and J. Henry Fitzgerald, to testify. Burns was a ballistics engineer for the United States Cartridge Company. He had worked there for thirty years. Fitzgerald was in charge of testing guns for the Colt Patent Firearms Company. Before that, he had worked for six years in the revolver department at the Iver Johnson Company.

Along with Captain Proctor and Captain Van Amberg, Burns test-fired Sacco's gun. Fitzgerald was not at these

IF IT HAD NOT BEEN FOR THESE THING,
I MIGHT HAVE LIVE OUT MY LIFE TALK-
ING AT STREET CORNERS TO SCORN-
ING MEN. I MIGHT HAVE DIE, UN-
MARKED, UNKNOWN A FAILURE. NOW
WE ARE NOT A FAILURE. THIS IS OUR
CAREER AND OUR TRIUMPH. NEVER IN
OUR FULL LIFE COULD WE HOPE TO
DO SUCH WORK FOR TOLERANCE, FOR
JOOSTICE, FOR MAN'S ONDERSTANDING
OF MAN AS NOW WE DO BY ACCIDENT.
OUR WORDS-OUR LIVES-OUR PAINS
NOTHING! THE TAKING OF OUR LIVES-
LIVES OF A GOOD SHOEMAKER AND A
POOR FISH PEDDLER-ALL! THAT LAST
MOMENT BELONGS TO US- THAT
AGONY IS OUR TRIUMPH.

One artist's impression of Sacco and Vanzetti while the two were handcuffed together. Below the drawing are statements by Vanzetti.

tests. At the trial, Burns was shown the six bullets test-fired from Sacco's gun, along with the third bullet that had been removed from Berardelli. The defense asked Burns if the six bullets had any of the same characteristics as the third bullet. Burns replied, "Not in my opinion. Bullet No. 3 doesn't compare at all with these six bullets."[8] (The six bullets did not have the same irregularity in markings when compared with the third bullet.)

Burns was then shown Vanzetti's gun. If Burns said this gun did not have a new hammer, then it could not be Berardelli's gun. No, Burns testified, the hammer was not new.

Like Burns, Fitzgerald said the third bullet had not been fired from Sacco's gun. He explained that the markings on the third bullet did not match the markings on the test bullets. This meant the Sacco's gun had not been used to fire the third bullet.

Fitzgerald also agreed with Burns that the hammer in Vanzetti's gun was the same age as the rest of the gun. According to both Burns and Fitzgerald, Vanzetti's gun did not have a new hammer. This meant, said the defense, that Vanzetti's gun was not Berardelli's gun.

Sacco's Alibi

On the day of the crime, Sacco was not at work. Where was he? Sacco claimed that on April 15, 1920, he was in Boston getting a passport at the Italian consulate. At midday, he had lunch and later, he had coffee with friends. The defense presented many witnesses to support his account. These witnesses included the clerk at the Italian consulate, his lunch friends, and Italian people he met at the train station or on the streets. Sacco said that he had taken the 8:56 A.M. train to get to Boston.

The defense called Angelo Monello to testify. Monello, a contractor for thirteen years, lived in Roxbury near Boston. Monello said that he saw Sacco on April 15, at about 11:00 A.M. They talked about a play, Sacco's passport, and the Italian consulate.

Felice Guadenagi testified that at 11:30 A.M. he met Sacco in front of Boni's restaurant. Guadenagi, had lived in Boston for seven years, and was a journalist. The two went into Boni's to eat. While they were in the restaurant, Guadenagi introduced Sacco to two friends, Albert Bosco and John D. Williams. These two men also testified for the defense. Both talked about meeting Sacco at Boni's and said that Sacco's passport had been a topic of conversation.

Sacco and Guadenagi left the restaurant at about 1:30 that afternoon. Alone, Sacco went back to the Italian consulate to get his passport. He could not get it because the photo he had brought for the passport was too large. Later, at 3:00 P.M., Sacco and Guadenagi again met to have coffee at Joe Giordano's coffeehouse. Guadenagi testified that he talked with Sacco about his passport and going to Italy at both meetings. While they were at the coffeehouse, Guadenagi introduced Sacco to Antonio Dentamore.

Dentamore, a Catholic priest, was in charge of exchanging foreign money at a bank. His testimony agreed with Sacco's and Guadenagi's.

Giuseppe Andrower was the clerk at the Italian consulate who talked with Sacco on April 15. Sacco, said Andrower, had brought a large photograph and because of its size, it could not be used to make a passport. Andrower remembered talking with Sacco on April 15 for three reasons: Sacco's photo had been too large, business was slow that day, and Andrower and his boss had laughed together about the unusually large photo. Andrower had also remembered the date because he had noticed a big calendar in his boss' office while talking with his boss.

Rosina Sacco, another witness, testified that her husband went to Boston on April 15. He had taken the big photo with him, but said Sacco came back with it and told her that the consulate had told him it was too large.

To discredit her testimony, the prosecution reminded the jury that immediately after his arrest, Sacco had claimed he was at work on April 15. Only later had Sacco's Boston alibi been brought out.

Vanzetti's Alibi

Thirteen witnesses either testified that Vanzetti was in Plymouth selling fish on April 15 or further supported his alibi. Vanzetti's alibi was that he was at his usual job as a fish peddler in Plymouth on April 15. "In the 15th of April is a day common to every other day to me. I peddled fish."[9] That morning, he sold fish from his cart until he ran out. He spent the afternoon chatting with Italian friends. A number of witnesses supported his alibi. Antonio Carbone, a

Plymouth fish dealer, testified that he had sold fish to Vanzetti just before April 15.

Angelo Guidobone who lived in Plymouth said he bought fish from Vanzetti on the morning of April 15. He placed the time at shortly after noon.

Joseph Rosen, a cloth peddler, testified that he saw Vanzetti in Plymouth selling fish from a pushcart. At about noon, Rosen approached Vanzetti who chose a piece of material for a suit. Rosen was able to remember the time because he heard the factory whistles blowing, as they did every work day at noon. Vanzetti took Rosen to a house about two blocks away to ask the woman there about the quality of the material. When the men entered the house, two women were there; one was younger than the other. Because Vanzetti and the two women spoke in Italian, Rosen could not understand their conversation. Finally, Vanzetti and Rosen left the house, returned to Vanzetti's cart, and bargained to reach a price. Vanzetti bought the cloth and Rosen left.

The house that Rosen visited was the Brini house. Sacco had rented a room from the Brinis for four years. Rosen identified Alfonsina Brini as the older woman he met on April 15. Through an interpreter, Mrs. Brini testified that Vanzetti and Rosen had come to her home at about 11:30 A.M. Vanzetti had shown her and her daughter, LeFavre Brini, a piece of cloth that he might buy from Rosen. Mrs. Brini recalled that she talked to Vanzetti and Rosen on April 15 because it was soon after her return from the hospital.

She also testified that Vanzetti had delivered fish to her house between 10:00 A.M. and 10:30 A.M. that same day.

LeFavre Brini was fifteen years old at the time of the trial. She backed up her mother's story. She remembered the date as April 15 for three reasons: She had stayed home from work to care for her mother on April 15; her father had requested a nurse for her mother also on that date; and her mother had called a doctor on April 14.

Melvin Corl, another witness, was a fisherman. He had known Vanzetti since 1915. Corl was painting his boat on the afternoon of April 15, when he and Vanzetti started talking at about 2:00 P.M. They talked for about an hour and a half. Corl remembered the date because he was planning to finish painting his boat on April 16.

During the question and answer exchange, the prosecution tried to show that Vanzetti's witnesses, including many friends, were not credible. The prosecution questioned the ability of the witnesses to recall dates and other important facts.

Not Guilty Behavior

Before and after their arrest, said the state, both men behaved as if they were guilty of the murders. To contradict this, the defense called Vanzetti, then Sacco, to the witness stand to testify. Each man would explain why he was armed and why he lied when questioned upon arrest.

The defense knew that Sacco's and Vanzetti's anarchist beliefs and activities would most likely prejudice the jury against them.[10] Yet to fully explain Sacco and Vanzetti's behavior, the defense had both men discuss their political views and activities. The Red Scare had been in full force when the two were arrested. Government activities against radicals produced great fear in both men—fear of the law, physical violence, and even of death.[11]

Vanzetti on the Witness Stand

By the afternoon of Tuesday, July 5, 1921, the temperature inside and outside the courtroom had soared. In this blistering heat, the defense called Vanzetti to testify. Vanzetti looked worn and tired as he sat in the witness stand. His eight months in jail had caused his hair to thin. But he was neatly dressed in a dark suit, black bow tie, and white shirt. Although he spoke with a heavy accent, he testified in English without an interpreter, and answered all questions asked by the defense and prosecution.

Vanzetti first described his years in Italy, then his thirteen years in the United States. He explained that he had gone to Mexico in 1917 because he did not support World War I. When he returned to America, he lived

In his analytical book about the Sacco and Vanzetti trial, Justice Felix Frankfurter questioned the fairness of the trial. A noted lawyer, Frankfurter later became a Justice of the United States Supreme Court.

in Plymouth with the Brini family and became a fish peddler. Vanzetti then detailed his activities from April 14 through his arrest on May 5.

During the cross-examination, the prosecution asked Vanzetti many questions about why he opposed World War I and lived in Mexico until the end of the war.

When asked why he owned a gun, Vanzetti said that he carried a lot of cash for his business and he carried a gun for protection. He explained, "There were many crimes, many hold-ups, many robberies at that time."[12]

Why had he, Sacco, and the others gone to get an automobile on May 5? Vanzetti testified that they needed one to haul books and newspapers. That night the men had planned to begin collecting a great deal of anarchist literature from various houses.

Vanzetti was now talking about activities in which he and his fellow radicals were involved. At this point, the entire courtroom was very quiet. Everyone present must have realized Vanzetti was talking about his "political views that were the equivalent of carrying and handling a bomb."[13]

He readily admitted to telling many lies after his arrest and during long question-and-answer sessions. He explained that he had lied to protect himself and his anarchist friends during the period of the Red Scare. Many of his friends had anarchist books and newspapers in their homes. If he had given the police the names and addresses of his friends, then they could have been arrested and perhaps jailed or returned to their native country. Vanzetti knew this could happen because he kept up with national and international news and political happenings of anarchists, socialists, and others with radical political views.

Sacco on the Witness Stand

Sacco was called to the witness stand on Thursday, July 7, 1921, another hot day. Sacco looked younger than Vanzetti and in better health. He was dressed in a dark suit and a black string tie. Although he did not express himself well in English, Sacco did not use an interpreter for most of his testimony.

Like Vanzetti, Sacco first talked about his years in Italy and of his decision to come to America. Then he described his years in America, including his arrest. He testified about going to Boston on April 15 to get an Italian passport.

When asked why he owned a gun, Sacco said that he was a night watchman for the 3K Shoe Factory and needed a gun. His employer had previously testified it was legitimate for a night watchman to have a gun.

Similar to Vanzetti's cross-examination, Sacco's draft dodging and time in Mexico was questioned. Like Vanzetti, Sacco explained that he did not support any war.

On July 8, the prosecution asked Sacco to again explain why he had come to America. Sacco then launched into a ten-minute speech. He said that in the United States, through hard work, he and his fellow workers could raise a family and give their children an education. Yet no matter how hard he and others tried, their dreams did not become reality. Their children could not go to high school or for higher education. Why? Poor people "can't live and send his child and go to Harvard College if he wants to eat," he said.[14] He concluded his speech about anarchism and socialism with, "I love Socialists."[15]

To some people in the courtroom, Sacco's speech sounded as if it was filled with hatred of the American government.[16] When Sacco finished, the entire courtroom was silent for a long time.

The prosecution then continued its cross-examination. Sacco readily admitted to lying after his arrest. Like, Vanzetti, he lied to protect his anarchist friends from possible arrest and deportation. After Sacco left the witness stand, Vanzetti's lawyers asked Judge Thayer if the two men could be tried separately. Vanzetti's lawyers were concerned that Sacco's speech about socialism and anarchism would prejudice the jury. If that was true, Vanzetti would most likely not get a fair verdict. The judge refused, saying that proper instructions to the jury would take care of this issue.

After a few more defense witnesses testified, the defense and prosecution gave their closing statements. During these long speeches, each side made final summaries of the facts and tried to discredit the other side's witnesses and evidence.

A total of 167 witnesses had testified during the long, emotional trial. Both sides had presented their cases to the jurors. Now, these twelve men would decide the fate of Sacco and Vanzetti.

chapter six

THE DECISION

COURT ROOM—On the morning of July 14, Judge Thayer began instructing the jury. Fifteen months had passed since the killings. Before the jury left the courtroom to consider its verdict, he told the jurors how the law applied to the case. He also asked them to follow his instructions to the best of their ability. He told the jury to consider only the evidence and testimony presented at the trial.

The Jury Deliberates

Judge Thayer's instructions had gone on for several hours. Now it was noon and the court broke for lunch. At 3:00 P.M., the jury went into a separate room. They took the physical evidence from the case with them, including the bullets. The deputy sheriff locked the door. No one was permitted to hear what was discussed in the jury room.

One of the jurors later wrote about what happened once the door was locked. He said that all twelve men had already made up their minds—Sacco and Vanzetti were guilty. But the men thought it would not look

Deliberating as a Juror

There is no set procedure that jurors must follow when deciding a case. Each jury decides how to hold discussions, settle differences of opinion, and vote. Many judges give jurors the following information:

- Jurors must discuss the evidence presented on all important issues before taking a vote on the verdict.

- Each juror should express his or her opinion during the deliberations.

- No juror should be pressured into changing a vote in order to arrive at a verdict more quickly.

- Each juror should weigh opposing views carefully.

- Any juror can change his or her vote if a discussion has caused a change of opinion.

right to deliver their verdict quickly, so they decided to stay in the jury room awhile.[1] First, the jurors took an informal poll. To start a discussion, two jurors voted that Sacco and Vanzetti were not guilty.[2]

Everyone then discussed the case. They handled the guns and bullets. About halfway through the afternoon, the jurors asked for a magnifying glass, which they were given.

The jurors continued to agree on the guilty verdicts. At 7:55 P.M., just after sunset, the deputy sheriff heard a triple knock at the jury room door. The jurors had reached a verdict.

The Verdicts

Sacco and Vanzetti and their lawyers stood. They listened as the clerk of the court said, "Mr. Foreman, look upon the prisoner. Prisoner, look upon the Foreman. What say you, Mr. Foreman, is the prisoner at the bar guilty or not guilty?"[3] Sacco heard his verdict first. He was found guilty.

Now it was Vanzetti's turn to hear his verdict. He, too, was declared guilty. Sacco stood and loudly said in Italian, "Sono innocente. Sono innocente." ["I am innocent. I am innocent."][4]

Rosina Sacco and friends of Sacco and Vanzetti began

Sacco and Vanzetti are shown leaving Dedham Courthouse after the sentencing. Vanzetti is wearing a light-colored hat in the front row of men. Sacco is directly to his right.

crying. Rosina Sacco broke through the line of guards surrounding the two men and embraced her husband. A police officer moved her away. The heavily guarded prisoners were returned to their prison cells.

The Verdicts Spark Controversy

When the jury returned the guilty verdicts, an immediate outcry arose from many people throughout the world. Many people felt that Sacco and Vanzetti did not get a fair trial and that they had been condemned because they were guilty of being Italians and anarchists—not because they were guilty of the murders. Judge Thayer and the jurors were accused of prejudice. In fact, the police put Judge Thayer's house under constant watch.

Around the world, protests and violence erupted over Sacco and Vanzetti's convictions. People in France, Italy, Belgium, Spain, Portugal, Switzerland, and Scandinavia staged protests. In France, thousands of French police prevented a mob from taking over the American embassy in Paris. Other American embassies and consulates in Europe and South America were flooded with letters of protest.

Justice Felix Frankfurter, a noted lawyer, later became a Justice of the United States Supreme Court. In his 1927 book, *The Case of Sacco and Vanzetti*, he wrote, that Judge Thayer's denial

> is literally honeycombed with demonstrable errors and infused by a spirit alien to justice or judicial utterance [speech]. With the cross-examination of Sacco and Vanzetti, patriotism and radicalism become the dominant emotional

issues. The prosecutor systematically played on the feelings of the jury by exploiting the unpatriotic and despised beliefs of Sacco and Vanzetti, and the judge allowed this.[5]

Lois B. Rantoul sat at Sacco's and Vanzetti's trial every day, except for one afternoon. She represented the Boston Federation of Churches. Like Frankfurter, Rantoul disagreed with the verdicts. In her final trial report, she said that little evidence was presented during the trial that showed Sacco and Vanzetti were guilty. Instead, they were convicted because the two men were anarchists who were against war. Based on the trial proceedings, she felt that "Sacco and Vanzetti [were] still innocent."[6]

The *Boston American*, a local newspaper, also disagreed with the guilty verdicts. It said, "Nearly all the newspaper reporters who covered this trial agree that the verdict of guilty was not justified."[7] Other local newspapers agreed with the editorial in the *Boston American*.

The Prisoners

After the verdicts, Sacco and Vanzetti were separated. Vanzetti was put into Charlestown Prison to serve time for the Bridgewater

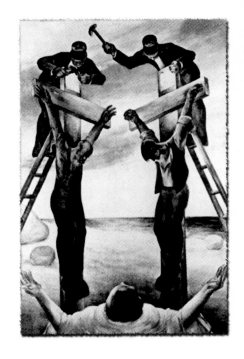

One artist's drawing depicted the verdict and upcoming execution of Sacco and Vanzetti and what it meant to the people of Massachusetts.

crime. Sacco stayed at the Dedham Prison. He had not yet received his sentence. Sacco and Vanzetti did not meet again for six years except for brief occasions, until they received their final sentencing—death sentences for both men—in the Dedham courthouse in 1927. (Appeals of the guilty verdicts lasted for six years, so Sacco and Vanzetti were not sentenced by Judge Thayer immediately after they were convicted.)

chapter seven

WHERE DO WE STAND TODAY?

JAIL HOUSE—Sacco's and Vanzetti's lawyers and supporters continued a lengthy legal fight to save the two men from their death sentences. From 1921 to 1927, a total of eight appeals were filed. An appeal is a legal request to review a case that has already gone through trial. In the end, the guilty verdicts remained for both men.

The Appeals

Two days after Sacco's and Vanzetti's trial ended, Fred Moore, chief lawyer for the defense, filed an appeal with the Massachusetts court. He tried to show that Sacco and Vanzetti were entitled to a new trial. To get a new trial, defense lawyers had to show that the defendants' rights had been violated, or produce new evidence that would affect the verdict. Moore claimed the evidence that had been presented at trial did not support the verdict.

Sacco's and Vanzetti's trial judge, Judge Thayer, scheduled the hearing for the new trial motion at

Dedham on October 29, 1921. During the 1920s, the laws of Massachusetts allowed the original trial judge to rule on appeals.

The courthouse was heavily guarded. State Troopers circled around on motorcycles and on horses. Inside, many police stood guard. Only forty spectators were allowed into the courtroom. After hearing Moore's appeal, Judge Thayer told the defendants that he would consider the question of whether a new trial should be held. On Christmas Eve, December 24, 1921, he denied Sacco and Vanzetti a new trial.

Over the next six years, Sacco's and Vanzetti's lawyers filed various appeals for a new trial. Each time, the lawyers produced new evidence to show that the verdict should be overturned. Judge Thayer heard and denied each appeal.

One of the appeal motions was filed when new evidence was uncovered in late 1925. At that time, Celestino F. Madeiros was in the same prison with Sacco. Madeiros had a long criminal history, but was in jail for a bungled bank robbery and murder. Through a jail messenger, on November 18, 1925, he sent a note to Sacco. He signed this note: "I hear by confess to being at the South Braintree shoe company crime and Sacco and Vanzetti were not in said crime."[1]

When questioned by Sacco's and Vanzetti's lawyers, Madeiros supplied a wealth of information about the robbery and murders of April 15, 1920. For example, he described all the men who were with him during the crime and supplied details about the holdup plan and actual events of the crime. Again Judge Thayer denied a new trial, saying that Madeiros was not telling the truth and that Madeiros had not committed the murder and robbery.

The Sentencings

In January 1926, lawyers for Sacco and Vanzetti made their final two appeals—to the Massachusetts Supreme Judicial Court—the highest court in the state. In the first appeal, Sacco's and Vanzetti's lawyers said that the guilty verdict was unjust. Judge Thayer had not followed the law when he allowed Sacco's cross-examination. The previous requests for appeals also clearly showed that a new trial was in order. The Court agreed with Judge Thayer's denial for a new trial.

Meanwhile, early in 1927, lawyers appealed to the United States Supreme Court, the highest court in the country. When Justice Oliver Wendell Holmes declined to hear the appeal, the other Supreme Court Justices backed his decision. In January 1927, the defense lawyers again appealed to the Massachusetts Supreme Judicial Court. This time, they asked that Madeiros's information be heard in a new trial. On April 5, 1927, the Court again agreed with Judge Thayer's denial for a new trial.

Four days later, Sacco, Vanzetti, and their lawyers stood before Judge Thayer. Judge Thayer sentenced both men to die by electrocution on Sunday, July 10, 1927. Sacco protested: "You condemn two innocent men."[2]

Governor of Massachusetts Investigates

Throughout the years of appeal requests, many people worldwide protested the convictions of Sacco and Vanzetti as unjust. Demonstrations were held in Russia, Japan, Hong Kong, Australia, Mexico, Chile, Cuba, Brazil, France, Italy, Scandinavia, Portugal, Spain, and Belgium. Sometimes the protests grew violent. Bombs and grenades exploded, and shootings occurred. In America, public officials in Massachusetts received telegrams and citizens wrote letters to the editors of newspapers, voicing their opposition to the convictions.

After Sacco and Vanzetti received their death sentences, millions of supporters appealed to Massachusetts governor Alvan Tufts Fuller to halt the executions. On June 1, 1927, Governor Fuller appointed a committee, to review the trial,

its motions for appeals, and denials. He selected three men for the committee—Abbott Lowell, president of Harvard University; Samuel Wesley Stratton, president of the Massachusetts Institute of Technology; and Robert Grant, a former judge. Since Lowell headed the commission, it was called the Lowell Commission.

The men reviewed the testimony and evidence presented at

In 1927 Chief Justice Oliver Wendell Holmes and the rest of the Justices on the Court declined to hear an appeal from Sacco and Vanzetti.

the trials and the requests for appeals. They interviewed more than one hundred witnesses, including those who had originally testified at the trial. The governor conducted his own investigation. He, too, went over the testimony given at the trial and the appeals process. He visited the crime scene and talked to Sacco and Vanzetti. No record exists of the governor's private study, so we do not know how and why he came to his own decision. We do know that the governor and the commission reviewed the entire case in just a few weeks. It is highly unlikely that these men could have thoroughly reviewed the thousands of pages of trial testimony and new evidence submitted for the appeals in such a short time.

On July 27, 1927, the Lowell Commission gave a twenty-page report to Governor Fuller. The commission concluded that Judge Thayer had been "indiscreet" at times.[3] However, "on the whole" Sacco and Vanzetti had received a fair trial, and they should be electrocuted for their crimes.[4] On August 3, 1927, Governor Fuller announced that he and the commission agreed: Sacco and Vanzetti's death sentences were to remain. He said, "I believe, with the jury, that these men, Sacco and Vanzetti, were guilty and that they had a fair trial."[5]

Final Days

Following Governor Fuller's announcement, riots broke out near American embassies worldwide. But these protests did not help the condemned men. In early August, both Sacco and Vanzetti went on a hunger strike for fifteen days, until they were threatened with forcible feeding.

On August 18, Sacco wrote a long, loving farewell letter to his son, Dante. At the end of the letter, he said,

> Dante, I say once more to love and be nearest to your mother and the beloved ones in these sad days, and I am sure that with your brave heart and kind goodness they will feel less discomfort. And you will also not forget to love me a little for I do—O, Sonny!
>
> Thinking so much and so often of you. Best fraternal greetings to all the beloved ones, love and kisses to your little Ines and mother. Most hearty affectionate embrace.[6]

Two days before their death, Sacco and Vanzetti wrote a final letter from the Massachusetts State Prison to thank their supporters:

> We have no hope [of a hold on their executions]. Therefore, we decided to write this letter to you to express our gratitude and admiration for all what you have done in our defense during these seven years, four months, and eleven days of struggle. That we lost and have to die does not diminish our appreciation and gratitude for your great solidarity with us and our families. Be all as of one heart in this blackest hour of our tragedy. And have heart.[7]

On the evening of August 22, 1927, both Sacco and Vanzetti were locked in Charlestown State Prison in separate cells. Five hundred armed police officers guarded the prison, breaking up protest marches that sprang up outside the prison.

Sacco died first. Just after midnight, he spoke his last words, "Long live anarchy! Farewell my wife and child and all my friends."[8] He died at 12:19.

Vanzetti's last words were, "I wish to say to you that I am innocent. I have never done a crime, some sins, but never any crime . . . I am an innocent man."[9] He died at 12:26.

A funeral procession was held on August 29. On that cold, misty afternoon, thousands walked or drove behind the hearses. Hundreds of thousands more watched from the sidewalks. Afterward, Sacco and Vanzetti were cremated.

Legal Violations

Over the years, historians and lawyers have analyzed the *Sacco and Vanzetti* case. Some have said that Judge Thayer and the prosecuting lawyers violated various legal codes, or

Massachusetts governor Alvan Tufts Fuller appointed a commission, or committee, to review the Sacco and Vanzetti *case.*

standards, of the American Bar Association. Some of these ABA codes, however, were established after 1921. Organized in 1878, the American Bar Association (ABA) promotes professional legal standards for its member lawyers. Lawyers who practice law in any state can become members of the ABA.

Both during the trial and during the appeals process, Judge Thayer reportedly made many prejudicial comments outside the courtroom about the defendants and their lawyers. At one point, when speaking about defense lawyer Fred H. Moore, he shouted, "I'll show them that no long-haired anarchist from California can run this court!"[10] Moore, an unconventional lawyer from California, had successfully defended radicals before taking Sacco's and Vanzetti's case.

On May 5, 1920, Sacco and Vanzetti were not told why they had been arrested, that they had a right to a lawyer, or that they did not have to answer questions. No lineup was used to identify witnesses. The information collected during these times was used unfairly as evidence at their trial.

Although Sacco's and Vanzetti's flight to Mexico and their antiwar beliefs were not relevant to the case, Judge Thayer allowed questions about both topics. The prosecution also made fun of Sacco's and Vanzetti's anarchist beliefs.[11]

The prosecutor tried to prejudice the jury against Sacco and Vanzetti by appealing to the jury's dislike of people who were opposed to war. These feelings were not only permitted, but also increased by Judge Thayer himself. For example, he instructed the jury to perform their duties "like the true soldier . . . responded to that call in the spirit of supreme American loyalty."[12]

Wrongfully Executed

More evidence was found after Sacco's and Vanzetti's deaths to suggest that their convictions had been unjust. According to an American Express receipt, Vanzetti, as he had testified, had received a shipment of eels on December 24, 1919. Also, none of the money stolen on April 15, 1920, was ever recovered or traced to Sacco and Vanzetti.

On August 23, 1977, fifty years to the day after the executions of Sacco and Vanzetti, Michael S. Dukakis, governor of Massachusetts, issued a proclamation. Dukakis apologized to Sacco and Vanzetti for their wrongful execution, but did not overturn (reverse) their convictions. Instead, the governor proclaimed that "any stigma and disgrace should be forever removed from the names of Nicola Sacco and Bartolomeo Vanzetti."[13] The proclamation also called for people to be careful "against our susceptibility to prejudice, our intolerance of unorthodox ideas and our failure to defend the rights of persons who are looked upon as strangers in our midst."[14]

Exactly twenty years after the proclamation, on August 23, 1997, Thomas Menino, mayor of Boston, paid tribute to Sacco and Vanzetti by accepting a bronze sculpture of the two men for the city. This memorial, he said, is "to remind us of the dangers of miscarried justice, and the right we all have to a fair trial."[15]

Continuing Controversy

Even with the 1977 proclamation, the case of *Sacco and Vanzetti* remains controversial. Many questions remain unanswered. For example, did Sacco and Vanzetti kill and rob Parmenter and Berardelli? According to many historians and legal experts, there is no clear answer. Historians Louis Joughin and Edmund M. Morgan wrote a book in 1948 that studied the impact of the case on American law, literature, and society. They agree there are no clear answers to the questions this case raises.[16]

In 1985, William Young and David E. Kaiser, wrote *Postmortem: New Evidence in the Case of Sacco and Vanzetti.* They spent more than a decade researching newly uncovered evidence about the case, and they concluded

that Sacco and Vanzetti were, in fact, innocent. The authors showed that Sacco and Vanzetti had been framed for two murders they had not committed, and that "virtually every piece of evidence against the two men ultimately rested on falsehoods and fabrications."[17]

On August 23, 1977, fifty years to the day after the executions of Sacco and Vanzetti, Governor Michael Dukakis of Massachusetts issued a proclamation to apologize to Sacco and Vanzetti for their wrongful execution.

People continue to question whether Sacco and Vanzetti were treated unfairly because of their political beliefs and the era. Historian Samuel Eliot Morison wrote in his book *The Oxford History of the American People*, "The Sacco and Vanzetti case was an offshoot of the whipped-up anti-red hysteria of the period just following World War I."[18] Professor Horace M. Kallen, in a 1929 article, agreed. He said, ". . . the ten years since the end of the Great War [WWI] exhibit an unequalled disintegration of the legal, the industrial, and the social morality of the State [of Massachusetts]."[19]

Hundreds of plays, operas, poems, songs, movies, videos, paintings, and books have been created about Sacco and Vanzetti. Each one continues the debate: Were these two Italian immigrants guilty of robbery and murder? Or were they victims because of their radical political beliefs?

Questions for Discussion

1. Why do you think the verdict in the *Sacco and Vanzetti* case has remained in question for so long?

2. Why do you think the *Sacco and Vanzetti* case has inspired so many people to create books, movies, plays, and songs?

3. In 1977 the governor of Massachusetts issued a proclamation that apologized for the wrongful deaths of Sacco and Vanzetti. He did not, however, overturn their convictions. What is the significance of this?

4. Do you think the police had enough probable cause to arrest Sacco and Vanzetti? Support your answer.

5. Defendants do not have to testify during their trial. Do you think it was a good idea for Sacco to testify? Support your answer. Do you think it was a good idea for Vanzetti to testify? Support your answer.

6. Did the defense lawyers use good judgment during the trial in having Sacco and Vanzetti talk about their political beliefs and activities? Support your answer.

7. Although both Sacco and Vanzetti spoke English poorly, why do you think the defense had them testify without an interpreter?

8. During the trial, some of the defense witnesses directly contradicted the prosecution witnesses. Why do you think witnesses can present such different versions of what they saw or heard involving a crime?

9. The trial of Sacco and Vanzetti took nearly seven weeks. Both sides presented a great deal of evidence and many witnesses. The jury took fewer than six hours to deliver a verdict in this case. Do you think this was enough time for them to discuss all the important testimony and evidence presented in the trial? Explain.

10. Should Sacco and Vanzetti have received separate trials? Why or why not?

11. Based on the information presented in this book, do you think Sacco was guilty or innocent? Do you think Vanzetti was guilty or innocent?

12. During the 1920s, the laws of Massachusetts allowed the trial judge to rule on appeals of cases that he or she had tried. Do you think this was fair to Sacco and Vanzetti? Explain. Do you think Sacco and Vanzetti should have been granted a new trial, with a new judge? Explain.

Chapter Notes

Chapter 1. The Arrest of Sacco and Vanzetti

1. Paul Avrich, *Sacco and Vanzetti: The Anarchist Background* (Princeton, N.J.: Princeton University Press, 1991), p. 199.

2. Frank M. D'Alessandro, *The Verdict of Sacco and Vanzetti* (New York: Jay Street Publishers, 1997), p. 77.

Chapter 2. America in the Early 1900s

1. James W. Loewen, *Lies My Teacher Told Me* (New York: Simon & Schuster, 1995), p. 30.

2. Ibid.

3. Paul Avrich, *Sacco and Vanzetti: The Anarchist Background* (Princeton, N.J.: Princeton University Press, 1991), p. 94.

4. Loewen, p. 30.

5. Ibid.

6. Avrich, p. 159.

7. Ibid., pp. 153–154.

8. Ibid., p. 155.

9. The Professional Education Group, *The Matter of Sacco and Vanzetti: An Ethical Dilemma* (Minnetonka, Minn.: The Professional Education Group, Inc., undated), pp. 1–2.

10. Ibid., p. 2.

11. Ibid.

12. Russell Aiuto, "Sacco and Vanzetti: The Real Men," June 16, 1998, <http://www.crimelibrary.com/sacco/saccowho.html> (July 28, 1999).

13. Ibid.

14. Nicola Sacco and Bartolomeo Vanzetti, *The Letters of Sacco and Vanzetti* (New York: Penguin Books, 1997), p. 12.

15. Ibid., p. 45.

16. Ibid., p. 73.

17. Avrich, p. 28

18. Ibid., p. 35.

19. Beltrando Brini, "Interview," Court TV Online, 1998, <http://staging.courttv.com/greattrials/sacco.vanzetti/brini.htm> (February 2, 1999).

20. Sacco and Vanzetti, p. 68.

21. Ibid., p. 274.

22. Avrich, pp. 56–57.

Chapter 3. The Road to Court

1. "The Trial," Court TV Online, 1998, <http://staging. courttv.com/greattrials/sacco.vanzetti/brini.htm> (February 2, 1999).

2. Brian Jackson, *The Black Flag: A Look Back at the Strange Case of Nicola Sacco and Bartolomeo Vanzetti* (Boston: Routledge & Kegan Paul, 1981), p. 14.

3. Ibid.

4. Felix Frankfurter, "The Case of Sacco and Vanzetti," *The Atlantic Monthly*, March 1927, <http://www.theatlantic.com/ unbound/flashbks/oj/frankff.html> (June 2, 1998).

5. Jackson, p. 14.

6. Ibid., p. 17.

7. "The Trial," Court TV Online, 1998, <http://staging. courttv.com/greatesttrials/sacco.vanzetti/brini.htm> (February 2, 1999).

8. Frank M. D'Alessandro, *The Verdict of Sacco and Vanzetti* (New York: Jay Street Publishers, 1997), p. 127.

9. Ibid., p. 130.

10. Felix Frankfurter, *The Case of Sacco and Vanzetti: A Critical Analysis for Lawyers and Laymen* (New York: Grosset & Dunlap, 1927), p. 43.

11. Katherine Anne Porter, *The Never-Ending Wrong* (Boston, Mass.: Little, Brown and Company, 1977), p. 6.

12. D'Alessandro, p. 123.

Chapter 4. The Case for Massachusetts

1. Doreen Rappaport, *The Sacco-Vanzetti Trial* (New York: HarperCollins, 1992), pp. 33–34.

2. Felix Frankfurter, *The Case of Sacco and Vanzetti: A Critical Analysis for Lawyers and Laymen* (New York: Grosset & Dunlap, 1927), p. 14.

3. Felix Frankfurter, "The Case of Sacco and Vanzetti," *The Atlantic Monthly*, March 1927, <http://www.theatlantic.com/atlantic/atlweb/flashbaks/oj/frankff.htm> (February 2, 1999).

4. Herbert B. Ehrmann, *The Case That Will Not End* (New York: Little, Brown and Company, 1969), p. 198.

5. Brian Jackson, *The Black Flag: A Look Back at the Strange Case of Nicola Sacco and Bartolomeo Vanzetti* (Boston: Routledge & Kegan Paul, 1981), p. 20.

6. Frankfurter, *The Case of Sacco and Vanzetti*, p. 16.

7. Jackson, p. 25.

8. The Professional Education Group, *The Matter of Sacco and Vanzetti: An Ethical Dilemma* (Minnetonka, Minn.: The Professional Education Group, Inc., undated), p. 10.

9. Louis Joughin and Edmund M. Morgan, *The Legacy of Sacco and Vanzetti* (Chicago: Quadrangle Books, 1964), p. 90.

10. Frankfurter, *The Case of Sacco and Vanzetti*, p. 26.

11. Frankfurter, "The Case of Sacco and Vanzetti," March 1927, <http://www.theatlantic.com/atlantic/atlweb/flashbaks/oj/frankff. htm> (February 2, 1999).

12. Joughin and Morgan, p. 72.

13. Jackson, p. 26.

14. Paul Avrich, *Sacco and Vanzetti: The Anarchist Background* (Princeton, N.J.: Princeton University Press, 1991), p. 203.

Chapter 5. The Case for Sacco and Vanzetti

1. Doreen Rappaport, *The Sacco-Vanzetti Trial* (New York: HarperCollins, 1992), pp. 75–76.

2. Ibid., 76.

3. Francis Russell, *Sacco & Vanzetti: The Case Resolved* (New York: Harper & Row, 1986), p. 119.

4. Herbert B. Ehrmann, *The Case That Will Not End* (New York: Little, Brown and Company, 1969), p. 193.

5. Ibid.

6. Ibid., p. 365.

7. Ibid.

8. Rappaport, p. 94.

9. Ehrmann, p. 332.

10. Louis Joughin and Edmund M. Morgan, *The Legacy of Sacco and Vanzetti* (Chicago: Quadrangle Books, 1964), p. 96.

11. Ibid.

12. Felix Frankfurter, *The Case of Sacco and Vanzetti: A Critical Analysis for Lawyers and Laymen* (New York: Grosset & Dunlap, 1927), p. 39.

13. Frank M. D'Alessandro, *The Verdict of Sacco and Vanzetti* (New York: Jay Street Publishers, 1997), p. 166.

14. Ehrmann, p. 316.

15. Francis Russell, *Sacco & Vanzetti: The Case Resolved* (New York: Harper & Row, 1986), p. 106.

16. D'Alessandro, p. 171.

Chapter 6. The Decision

1. Francis Russell, *Sacco & Vanzetti: The Case Resolved* (New York: Harper & Row, 1986), p. 107.

2. Ibid.

3. Ibid.

4. Brian Jackson, *The Black Flag: A Look Back at the Strange Case of Nicola Sacco and Bartolomeo Vanzetti* (Boston: Routledge & Kegan Paul, 1981), pp. 47–48.

5. Felix Frankfurter, *The Case of Sacco and Vanzetti: A Critical Analysis for Lawyers and Laymen* (New York: Grosset & Dunlap, 1927), p. 46.

6. Frank M. D'Alessandro, *The Verdict of Sacco and Vanzetti* (New York: Jay Street Publishers, 1997), p. 176.

7. Ibid., p. 179.

Chapter 7. Where Do We Stand Today?

1. Felix Frankfurter, "The Case of Sacco and Vanzetti," *The Atlantic Monthly*, March 1927, <http://www.theatlantic.com/atlantic/atlweb/flashbks/oj/frankff.htm> (February 2, 1999).

2. Brian Jackson, *The Black Flag: A Look Back at the Strange Case of Nicola Sacco and Bartolomeo Vanzetti* (Boston: Routledge & Kegan Paul, 1981), p. 68.

3. Michael E. Parrish, *Anxious Decades: America in Prosperity and Depression, 1920–1941* (New York: W. W. Norton & Company, 1992), p. 200.

4. Robert D'Attilio, "Sacco-Vanzetti Case (Overview)," August 13, 1996, <http:www.english.upenn.edu/~afilreis/88/scavan.html> (February 2, 1999).

5. Jackson, p. 76.

6. Nicola Sacco and Bartolomeo Vanzetti, *The Letters of Sacco and Vanzetti* (New York: Penguin Books, 1997), p. 74.

7. Ibid., pp. 320–321.

8. Russell Aiuto, "Sacco and Vanzetti: The Legacy of Sacco and Vanzetti," June 16, 1998, <http://www.crimelibrary.com/sacco/saccowho.html> (February 2, 1999).

9. Ibid.

10. Jackson., p. 194.

11. Ibid., 190.

12. Parrish, p. 200.

13. Jackson, p. 191.

14. "Their Legacy," Court TV Online, 1998, <http://staging.courttv.com/greatesttrials/sacco.vanzetti/polenberg.htm> (February 2, 1999).

15. Bill Porter, "Menino Honors Sacco, Vanzetti," *The Standard Times*, August 23, 1997, <http://www.s-t.com/daily/08-97/08-23-97/a03sr025.htm> (February 2, 1999).

16. Louis Joughin and Edmund M. Morgan, *The Legacy of Sacco and Vanzetti* (Chicago: Quadrangle Books, 1964), p. 505.

17. William Young and David E. Kaiser, *Postmortem: New Evidence in the Case of Sacco and Vanzetti* (Amherst, Mass.: The University of Massachusetts Press, 1985), p. 158.

18. Samuel Eliot Morison, *The Oxford History of the American People* (New York: Oxford University Press, 1965), p. 884.

19. Joughin and Morgan, p. 508.

Glossary

alibi—A reason a defendant gives for why he or she could not have done what he or she is accused of doing. This is usually a statement by a witness that the defendant was someplace else at the time of the crime.

alien—A person who is not a citizen of the country in which he or she lives.

amendment—New provisions or changes to the Constitution of the United States.

anarchist—Someone who is opposed to any type of government, believing that government is harmful and unnecessary.

appeal—Asking a court to review its decision or to hold a new trial based on new evidence; or asking a court with a greater authority to review the decision of a lower court.

Bill of Rights—The first ten amendments to the United States Constitution. The Bill of Rights gives Americans many freedoms and protections such as freedom of religion, speech, and the press.

burden of proof—The amount of evidence required in a case in order for a jury to find in favor of the person bringing the lawsuit. The more serious the consequences of the case, the greater the amount of proof is required.

closing arguments—At the end of the testimony, the lawyers for each side sum up what they believe the jury's verdict should be and why.

communists—People who advocate the elimination of private property and support common ownership and shared labor. Communists are sometimes called Reds.

criminal case—A legal action started by a state or federal prosecutor in the name of the state or United States asking for a punishment against a person accused of committing a crime.

cross-examination—Questioning of a witness by the opposing side's lawyer.

defendant—A person on trial who is accused of a crime.

defense lawyer—A lawyer who acts on behalf of a defendant on trial.

deliberations—A jury's discussion and evaluation of the evidence presented in a trial.

deportation—Return of immigrants or aliens to their native country.

evidence—Any statement or object presented in a court case as a proof of fact.

expert witness—A person who has specialized knowledge or experience in some area who can testify as a recognized authority.

foreperson—The leader on a jury. This person leads or organizes the discussion of a jury and is responsible for trying to keep order.

grand jury—A jury that investigates criminal complaints and decides whether someone should be formally charged with committing a crime.

immigrant—A person who settles in a country different from the one in which he or she was born.

indictment—A formal written accusation prepared for a court by a grand jury. It outlines what crime or crimes are believed to have been committed and names the person or persons who probably committed those crimes.

jury—A group of people who have sworn to decide the facts in a court case and to reach a fair verdict or decision.

Justice Department—Part of the executive branch of the federal government. This department handles cases in federal matters and interprets and enforces federal laws.

opening statements—The presentations made by the lawyers on both sides of the case at the start of a trial. During opening statements, the issues and facts that will be presented are outlined. The purpose of the opening statements is to give the jury an overview of the case and help the jury understand the evidence.

prosecutor—A government official authorized to accuse and prosecute (bring to trial) someone who is believed to have committed a crime. Prosecutors are known by various names in different parts of the United States. District attorney, state's attorney, and people's attorney are just a few examples.

radicals—People who are in favor of extreme measures to retain, restore, or overthrow an existing government.

Red Scare—The period from 1919 to 1920 in the United States when the civil rights of some groups of people were suppressed. These people, including Communists, socialists, and anarchists, were often arrested without search warrants and not given lawyers.

sentence—In criminal cases, the decision by a jury or judge assigning punishment to a convicted defendant.

socialism—A doctrine or movement calling for public ownership of factories and other means of production.

suspect—Someone who is thought to have been involved in a crime.

testimony—Evidence given after taking an oath in court to tell the truth; questions answered under oath concerning what one knows about a case being heard in court.

verdict—The decision that a jury or judge makes after hearing and considering all the evidence and testimony in a case.

witness—Someone who has seen or heard something relating to a crime; someone who provides evidence about something in a court.

Further Reading

D'Alessandro, Frank M. *The Verdict of Sacco and Vanzetti.* New York: Jay Street Publishers, 1997.

Rappaport, Doreen. *The Sacco-Vanzetti Trial.* New York: HarperCollins, 1992.

Sacco, Nicola and Bartolomeo Vanzetti. *The Letters of Sacco and Vanzetti.* New York: Penguin Books, 1997.

Sonn, Richard D. *Anarchism.* Old Tappan, N.J.: Macmillan Library Reference, 1992.

Internet Addresses

Court TV, "The Trial of Sacco and Vanzetti," <http://www.courttv.com/greatesttrials/sacco.vanzetti>

Felix Frankfurter, "The Case of Sacco and Vanzetti," *The Atlantic Monthly*, March 1927, <http://www.theatlantic.com/unbound/flashbks/oj/frankff.htm>

Katherine Ann Porter, "The Never-Ending Wrong," *The Atlantic Monthly*, June 1977, <http://www.theatlantic.com/unbound/flashbks/oj/porterf.html>

"The Trial of Sacco and Vanzetti," <http://www.msu.edu/course/mc/112/1920s/sacco-vanzetti/>

Infoplease.com Kids' Almanac, "The Sacco-Vanzetti Case," <http://lycoskids/infoplease.com/spot/saccovanzetti.html>

Index

A

Amendments to the United States Constitution,
Eighth, 33
Fifth, 32
Fourth, 32
Sixth, 32–33
American Civil Liberties Union, 38
anarchists, 10, 13–14, 15–16, 20, 22–23, 24–25, 37–38, 74–76
Andrews, Lola R., 45, 47–48, 64–65
Andrower, Giuseppe, 72
Arrogni, H., 65, 66
Avrich, Paul, 56

B

Berardelli, Alessandro, 7–8, 28, 34, 44, 49–50, 53
Berardelli, Mrs., 54
Bill of Rights, 32
Bolsheviks, 12
Bosco, Albert, 71
Brenner, William, 63
Brini, Alfonsina, 73–74
Brini, Beltrando, 21
Brini, LeFavre, 74
Brooks, Edward, 68
Burke, Frank, 61
Burlingame, Sergeant, 15
Burns, James, 68, 70

C

Callahan, William J., 59, 60
Campbell, Julia, 64
Carbone, Antonio, 72–73
Carter, Edward, 67–68
Cash, Harry, 68
Cerror, Henry, 62
Collins, Timothy J., 66–67
Constantino, Dominic, 63
Constitution, United States, 10, 31
Corl, Melvin, 74
Creel Committee on Public Information, 14
criminal case, steps of, 30–31, 41–43, 59
criminals, rights of, 31–33

D

Damato, N., 65, 66
Dentamore, Antonio, 71
Devlin, Frances, 45, 46
Dolbeare, Harry E., 52
Dukakis, Michael S., 93

E

Espionage Act of 1917, 14

F

Falcone, Emilio, 62
Faulkner, John W., 53, 68
Fay, George W., 65
Fitzgerald, J. Henry, 69, 70
Fitzemeyer, George F., 55–56
Fraher, Thomas F., 62–63
Frankfurter, Justice Felix, 82–83
Frantello, Albert, 61
Fuller, Alvan Tufts, 88–89

G

Gatti, Nicola, 62
Goodridge, Carlos E., 45, 48,
    65–66
grand jury, 30–31, 33–34
Grant, Robert, 88
Guadenagi, Felice, 71

H

Holmes, Justice Oliver Wendell,
    87

I

Immigration Act of 1918, 17
Iscorla, Pedro, 62
Italian Consulate, 23

J

Johnson, Mrs. Simon, 9
Jones, Mr., 54
Joughin, Louis, 94
jury
    decision, 79–81
    selection, 35–37

K

Kaiser, David E., 94
Kallen, Horace M., 95
Katzmann, District Attorney
    Frederick, 26–27, 43, 47, 49
Kelly, Michael, 19, 23, 49
Kurlansky, Harry, 64–65

L

Labrecque, Alfred, 65
LeVangie, Michael, 52, 66–68
Lowell, Abbott, 88

M

Madeiros, Celestino F., 86–87
Magazu, Peter, 65, 66
Manganaro, Andrew, 65
Massachusetts Supreme Judicial
    Court, 87
McAnarney, Jeremiah, 43, 59
McAnarney, Thomas F., 43, 59
McCarthy, Henry, 67

McCullum, 63–64
McNaught, Henry, 68
Menino, Thomas, 93
Monello, Angelo, 71
Moore, Fred, 43, 59, 85, 92
Morgan, Edmund M., 94
Morison, Samuel Eliot, 95

P

Palmer, Attorney General
    Mitchell, 14, 15, 16–17
Parmenter, Frederick A., 7–8, 28,
    34, 44
Pelzer, Louis, 45, 46–47, 63–64
Pierce, Winfred, 61
Porter, Katherine Anne, 38
Pratt, Ernest, 68
Proctor, Captain William H.,
    50–52, 68

R

Rantoul, Lois B., 83
Red Scare, 10, 16, 22–23, 24, 37,
    75, 76
Reed, Austin T., 52–53
Ripley, Walter, 37
Rose, Joseph, 73–74

S

Sacco, Dante, 19–20, 90
Sacco, Ines, 19
Sacco, Nicola, 11, 17, 18
    appeals, 85–89
    arrest, 9–10, 23, 24–25, 44, 78
    death, 90–91, 93
    early history, 19–20, 22–23
    political beliefs, 10, 17, 19,
        20–23, 24–26, 74–75,
        77–78, 90, 92, 95
    pretrial events, 24–28, 30,
        33–35, 38–40
    proclamation, state of
        Massachusetts, 93–94
    trial defense,
        alibi, 60, 70–72

not guilty behavior, 74–75, 77–78
strategy, 59–60
witnesses, 61–66, 77–78
trial evidence,
cap, 8, 43, 49
gun (pistol) and bullets, 9, 25
trial legal violations, 91–93
trial prosecution,
guilty behavior, 43, 56–57
strategy, 43
witnesses, 44–52
trial sentencing, 84, 87, 88–89
trial verdict, 79–80
Sacco, Rosina, 19, 72, 81–82
Salsedo, Andrew, 23, 39
Sedition Act of 1918, 14
Splaine, Mary F., 45–46, 62–63
Stewart, Chief Michael, 8, 25–27, 57
Stratton, Samuel Wesley, 88

T
Thayer, Judge Webster, 29, 33, 34–37, 78, 79, 84, 85–87, 89, 91–93
Trading-With-the-Enemy Act of 1917, 14

U
United States Supreme Court, 82, 87

V
Van Amburgh, Captain Charles, 51–52, 68
Vanzetti, Bartolomeo, 11, 17, 19
appeals, 85–89
arrest, 9–10, 23, 24–25, 44, 78
Bridgewater case, 28–30
death, 90–91, 93

early history, 20–23
political beliefs, 10,17, 19,21–23, 24–26, 74–77, 92, 95
pretrial events, 24–28, 30, 33–35, 38–40
proclamation, state of Massachusetts, 93–94
trial defense,
alibi, 60, 72–74
not guilty behavior, 74–78
strategy, 59–60
witnesses, 61–66, 77–78
trial evidence,
cap, 8, 43, 49
gun (pistol) and bullets, 9, 25, 27, 28, 39, 43, 44, 53, 54–55
trial legal violations, 91–93
trial prosecution,
guilty behavior, 43, 56–57
strategy, 43
witnesses, 44–52
trial sentencing, 84, 87, 88–89
trial verdict, 79–80
Victorson, Alexander G., 67

W
Wadesworth, Mr., 53–54
Williams, Assistant Attorney Harold, 43, 44
Williams, John D., 71
Wilson, President Woodrow, 12, 14
World War I, 11–12, 14, 20, 21, 75–76, 95

Y
Young, William, 94